Stephen Sharang, Ph.D., CPA

The Business of Consulting

What You Need to Know to Become a Highly Sought After Specialist

ISBN: 1-4392-4900-8
ISBN-13: 9781439249000

To order additional copies, please contact us.
BookSurge
www.booksurge.com
1-866-308-6235
orders@booksurge.com

DEDICATION

This book is dedicated to all who aspire to be self reliant and to God Almighty for His guidance and inspirction.

Contents

Chapter 1.   What Business is all about?   1

Defining Business   3
Reasons why People go into Business   4
Basic Requirements for starting a Business   5
Process and Banking Technology   6
Strategic Alliances   7
How to keep Overheads Low   8
Signs indicating the need for the Serv ces of a
Consultant   8

Chapter 2.   The Legal Structure of a Consulting Business 19

-The Sole Proprietorship   19
-The Partnership   21
-The Corporation   25
-The S Corporation   26

Chapter 3.   Finding Solutions to Problems in a
              Professional Way   29

-What is consulting?   29
-Who is a Management Consultant?   30
-Independent Consulting   31
-Qualities of a Good Consultant   31
-Types of Consulting Firms   32
-Scope of Consulting   33
-Requirement for succeeding in consulting   35
-How to Solve any Problem   36

Chapter 4.   Financing your Consulting Business   41

-Factors to Consider in Choosing a Means of Finance   41
-Main ways of Financing a Business   42

a.   Internal Sources   42
b.   External Sources   45

Chapter 5.   Effective Research on Consulting Projects   49

-Methods of Data Collection   49
Primary sources   50

a.   Interview   50
b.   Questionnaires   52
c.   Observation   53

Secondary Data   55

a. Internal Secondary Data Sources   55
b. External Sources of Data   55

Chapter 6.   Preparing and Making your Interview
             a success   57
-Suggestions for Ensuring that the Essentials are
 captured during the initial Interview   58
-7 Problem Areas to Address   60

Chapter 7.   Sharpening your Negotiating Skills   63

- Criteria for Negotiations   63
- Key Elements of a Good Negotiation   64
- Proven Techniques for Negotiating and Resolving
  Conflicts   66

- Parties to a Negotiation   68
- Conducting a Telephone Negotiation   69
- When a Negotiation is Considered Successful   69
- Negotiating for a Better Deal   70
- Winning a Negotiation   72
-Emotion and its Impact on Negotiations   73

Chapter 8   The Place of Ethics in Consulting and
                     Professional Practices   77

- Importance of Ethics to Consulting Practices   77
- Misconceptions about Ethics   78
- Codes of Ethics in Research   80
- The Purpose of Ethics   81
- Relativism Vs Stakeholder's theory   82
- Stakeholder's Theory   85
- Catering for all Interest Groups   87
- Corporate Governance   89
- Why Corporate Governance is Important   92

Chapter 9.   How to Manage and Influence People   93

- Functions of Management   93
-Planning;   94
-Directing;   94

Leadership-Ralph Waldo Emerson, Norman Vincent
    Peale, Stephen R. Covey,   95

Motivation-Abraham Irvin Maslow's Hierarchy of needs
theory, Victor Vroom's Expectancy theory, Frederick
Herzberg's two factor theory

-Why People Behave the Way they Do   101

- How to Manage Interpersonal Relationship   102

Chapter 10.   How Organisation's put their Affairs
              in Order   105

-Organizing (Coordination);   105
Division of Labour,   105
Departmentation,   105
Delegation of Duties, Span of Control.   106

Staffing;   107

Finding the Right Calibre of Staff,   107
Qualities of a Prospective Employee,   107
Terms of Employment in Bureaucratic Organisations,   108
Evaluating Employee and Organisational Performance, 109
Criteria for Measuring Public Sector Performance   110

Control; Characteristics of the Control Process   112
-Frederick Taylor and the Scientific Management
  Theory   113
-Process Design   114

Benchmarking;   115
Key steps to successful benchmarking,   115
Importance of benchmarking,   116
Areas where Benchmarking should focus on,   116
Benchmarking fails when: 117

Chapter 11.   Total Quality Management & Six SIGMA   119

- Origin of TQM   120
- Benefits of TQM   120
- Principle on Which TQM is based   121
- Six sigma   124

- Benefits of Six-Sigma to a Business   125

Chapter 12.   Strategic Planning for Consulting Firms   129

-Reasons to Make Strategies   130
-Qualities of a Good Strategy   130
-Strategic Management (Business strategy)   131
-Strategic Planning   132
-Contents of a Strategic Plan   132
-Scope of Strategic Planning   134
-Levels of Strategy   135
-The Seven -S- Model   136

Chapter 13.   Proposals: Stating Terms and Conditions
           of the Consulting Engagement   141

- Why a Proposal is Necessary   141
- Structure of a Good Proposal   140
- How to convert a Proposal into a Contract   142
- Accountants   146
- Attorneys   146

Chapter 14.   What you must know about Consulting
           Contract   149

- Why a Consulting Contract is necessary   151
- Choosing the form of Contract to adopt   151
- How to enter into a Contractual obligation   152
- Main types of Contracts in Consulting   153
- Basic Elements required in any Contract   156

Chapter 15. Making Professional Presentations &
           Communicating Effectively   159

- Why Communication is important to an Organization   161
- What is a Presentation?   161

- The Purpose of Presentations   161
- Keys to Effective Presentation   162
- Dealing with Stage Fright   169

Chapter 16.   Marketing Products and Services   171

- What Management is about   171
- Exchange of Goods and Services   172
- Relationship Marketing   173
- Growing Products/ Services and Creating
   More Business   175
- Focusing on the Intangibles   176

Chapter 17.   The Concept of Marketing Mix   179

- Key pricing Strategies for your Consulting Firm   180
- Adjusting Prices for Clients   182
- How to Bill your Client   183
- Promotion   185

Chapter 18. Creating Publicity for what you do   187

- The Remaining 3P's of Marketing   187
- Distribution-Getting Service to Clients   189
- Marketing Plan and Why it is Important   191
- Branding Products and Services   193
-Direct and Indirect Marketing   194
- Personal Selling   194
- Indirect Marketing   195
- Premiums   196
- Guerrilla marketing   196

Chapter 19. Use of IT, computers & the Internet   199

-Information age and Information Technology   200
-What would it Cost to acquire a Standard Technology
   for Personal or Business use?   200
-Hardware   201
-Software   203
-Why having a Website is Important   206
-Researching the Internet   206

Acknowledgement

There are many people I would like to thank for their inspiration, encouragement, and contributions to this project. Without their help and support, this book would not have been possible. My thanks go to the Management and staff of the Embassy of Nigeria Brussels, particularly Mr. Ahmed Nazimuddin, Mr. Toyin Alaka and Mrs. Felicia Emesiri for their encouragement constructive suggestions and also to all my friends too numerous to mention from all works of life. Finally, my deepest gratitude goes out to my wife Aine and my family for all the love and support during those times that I had to be unavoidably absent as a result of writing this book. Thank you from the bottom of my heart.

A Word from the Author

The contents of this book have been well researched and are an expression of the Author's desire to contribute to existing store of knowledge.

Disclaimer

This book is designed to provide information about the subject matter covered. It is sold with the understanding that the publisher and author are not engaged in rendering legal, psychological, or other professional services. If expert assistance is required, the services of a competent professional should be sought.

Every effort has been made to make this book as complete and accurate as possible. However, there may be mistakes both typographical and in content. Therefore, this text should be used only as a general guide.

The purpose of this book is to educate and entertain. The author and Publisher shall have neither liability nor responsibility to any person or entity with respect to any loss or damage caused or alleged to be caused directly or indirectly by the information contained herein.

Introduction

The book in your hand was conceived to be a guide for people seeking opportunities to use their skills and talents in a specialist way to help other people to solve their problems, whether in their private lives or business.

The author's objective is to help aspiring and practicing consultants to carry out their consulting engagements in an efficient and professional manner.

The author has also drawn inspiration from relevant aspects of his books the *"The Administration of a Business: Growth Strategies for the Development and Survival of Today's Corporate Organisations"* and *Managing Public Organisations: Understanding Financial Reporting and Policy Making in Processes of Government* where shared benefits exist.

It is organised into 19 chapters covering the following topics:

1. What Business is all about?
2. The Legal Structure of a Consulting Business
3. Finding Solutions to Problems in a Professional Way
4. Financing your Consulting Business
5. Effective Research on Consulting Projects
6. Preparing and Making your Interview a success
7. Sharpening your Negotiating Skills
8. The Place of Ethics in Consulting and Professional Practices

9. How to Manage and Influence People
10. How an Organisation can put its Affairs in Order
11. Total Quality Management & Six SIGMA
12. Strategic Planning for Consulting Firms
13. Use of IT, computers & the Internet
14. Proposals: Stating Terms and Conditions of the Consulting Engagement
15. What you must know about Consulting Contract
16. Making Professional Presentations & Communicating Effectively
17. Marketing Products and Services
18. The Concept of Marketing Mix
19. Creating Publicity for what you do

The book is a straight-forward, easy-to-read guide, guaranteed to influence the thought processes of the reader in a way that compels him to take action, avoid procrastination and to act, talk, and speak like a thoroughly bred professional who is confident and competent to undertake any consulting engagement.

Thus, all that is required to get started by anyone considering breaking into consulting to avoid the common mistakes often by those first starting out are examined to a sufficient depth. Those already consulting can also get an injection of fresh ideas for better service delivery to their clients.

Chapter 1
What Business is all about?

Your aspiration to become a consultant is a noble one. However, there are certain things you should know before you can become a highly sought after specialist. I give the 3 basic things to know to get you on your way to being all that you so greatly desire to become.

1.   Understand the nature and purpose of business

In order to have a firm grip, the right place to begin is to seek an understanding of what business is all about, because without this, you may never appreciate what is involved or required to become an effective and successful consultant.

2.   Understand that business is about People

Business is about people and not about you or your aspirations or ego because people become clients who in-turn keep your business open. It is crucially important to have the right motivation before venturing into any business to prevent a situation of regrets at the end of the day

3.   Think like an Entrepreneur

Entrepreneurship; often referred to as the fourth factor of production is the element that ties the other factors of production (land, labor, capital) together. Entrepreneurship is involved wherever someone through insight sees and takes an opportunity where others would ordinarily not dare. The opportunity may involve taking risks and burning bridges without providing for an escape route in order to ensure the success of a business or other similar ventures.

The entrepreneur then is not always someone that creates the new product or service; but the one who has the vision of how an idea can be translated into a vision for the benefit of every one. His skill or expertise shows up where finding the right market for products and services is the target, and also in presenting a service in a manner that is beneficial to a wider market and by implication a larger population. For instance, suppose Mr. X. owns a shop where he sells cloths basically produced by him, he may be doing well, but an entrepreneur is that person that can see beyond what the owner of the cloths sees at the moment. It is the entrepreneur that on invitation comes with a blueprint for turning that simple clothing shop into a more improved and widely marketed and sought after service by clients.

Thus, an entrepreneur is able to achieve a high rate of success through a combination of the elements of risks and rewards.

- Risk -because without this element he may not be an entrepreneur after all. By taking risks he is able to exert his business abilities to the utmost in order to achieve the desired end.

- Rewards—because he is aware that people respond by buying more products or services when there is a promise of a reward than when they are threatened with punishment.

To be a successful Consultant (entrepreneur) therefore, you will require certain attributes:

i.   Insight-the ability to see what others have missed;
ii.   Vision- the ability to make connections between things that others have not;
iii.   Creativity-the ability to create something unique, using the other three factors of production;
iv.   Business Sense-the ability to successfully market a product or service to society.

Defining Business

According to US Bureau of labour and statistics and Bureau of Census's Basic Monthly Survey, a business exists when the following among others are in place:

i)   Machinery or equipment of substantial value is being used in conducting the business, or
ii)   An office, store, or other place of business is being maintained, or
iii)   The business is advertised by:

1.   Listing in classified section of the telephone book, or
2.   Displaying a sign, or
3.   Distributing cards or leaflets or otherwise publicizing that the work or service is offered to the general public.

In other words, an activity is only recognised as a business if it has fulfilled all prescribed legal requirements of the country, state, region, municipal authority etc; wherein the investor operates. These requirements are basic to incorporating a business in many countries. In Nigeria for example, all matters on formation and incorporation of companies are regulated by the Companies and Allied Matters Act (The Company Act), while the Administration of the Com-

panies act is superintended over by the Corporate Affairs
Commission (CAC) whose functions include:

i)   The regulation and supervision of the formation, incor-
       poration, registration, management and winding up of
       companies;
ii)   The conduct of investigation into the affairs of any com-
       pany in the interest of shareholders and the public;
iii)   The maintenance of companies' registry.

   In addition to the above a company is required among
others; to disclose on its letter- head papers used in corre-
spondence, these particulars;

I)   Name of company/enterprise;
ii)   Address;
iii)   Registration /incorporation number;
iv)   Name of directors and alternate directors (if any).

Reasons why people go into business

1.   Being your own Boss

   Being one's boss is one of the biggest reasons why people go into business. To be one's own boss is to call the shots
and to determine the direction, remuneration and pace
for the company. However, it is not all that rosy or easy to
actualize in the sense that you become responsible for the
failure or otherwise of your company. Being your own boss
brings with it a sense of fulfillment.

2.   To make money

   Perhaps this is not a right motivation. But it does provide
an impetus for why people venture into business. The anticipated rewards to be made out of the business serves as

a catalyst for the entrepreneur and consequently propels him to establishing or going into business. It is quite obvious that, money can be made in business but this should not be your sole purpose for venturing into it as you may become frustrated in the event things do not turn out as early and as quickly as expected as a new business may take some time to begin yielding profits. My counsel is to apply patience and proper strategic thinking to doing business and in no time things may turn out as you initially anticipated.

Ego trip

It is very possible for people to start businesses just so that they can be seen as owning their own companies and be referred to as CEO(s). While some may succeed, the same cannot be said for others as the motivation for start-ing anything usually plays a big role in its success or failure.

To deliver a service

This to my mind is a better reason for going into or start-ing a business because business is not about making mon-ey or going on an ego trip, business is about delivery of ser-vice. Business is about people and how to meet their needs first and only thereafter can a claim be made to having the right to make money or gain financially from a business.

Requirements for starting a business

The basic requirement for starting a business in today's technology driven global business environment is quite sim-ple and not as expensive as one would suppose. Following are 2 basic requirements:

a).   A Computer- A computer is a high speed device that manipulates data according to c list of instructions.

b). A Bank Account-in the US an Employee Identification Number.

Process and Banking Technology

Banks and financial institutions invest heavily in technology and a wise business will exploit the use of these technologies to its advantage to enable it globalize easily. Some banks help a business keep a track of its transactions through online access to required information which can be downloaded to any financial software such as Microsoft Excel, lotus 1-2-3, Quick-Books etc.

In addition, there is also the benefit of doing business on-line for such things as posting and mailing a letter; through e-mail free of charge.

A business bank account will therefore enable businesses have access to:

i.   Bank contact or debit cards, credit cards and or cheque books.
ii.   Online statement;
iii. The ability to download transactions etc. online banking enables a business to optimize its process in a big way.

In his book *Stop Working, Rohan Hall* opines that a business' financial structure as a result of using technology developed by others (banks, financial institutions) would be made up as follows:

Technology infrastructures	cost
Computer	500
Printer, Fax	150
Financial software	100
24 hr access	0

Debit cards	0
24 hrs on-line help	0
On-line bill payment	0
Total technology	0
Total Technology Investment	$750

In other words, the financial requirement or infrastructure for starting a business using the benefits of strategic alliance or partnership will cost almost next to nothing, just about $750! In any case the cost could be much less if you already own a computer, an all in one printer/fax machine and financial software (sometimes comes with your computer package inbuilt) Imagine what the cost to get started would then be! It would be $0. (Zero)

In addition, Clients now accept/use credit and debit cards such as Master, Visa, Maestro cards etc. which signify that they have been verified before being given one. The advantage is that the billing company can help collect consulting fees on behalf of a company (without the business itself being the collection agency for a fee).

Strategic Alliances

A strategic alliance is a form of partnership whereby businesses based on their areas of core competencies join forces with others in carrying out their business. It has the advantages of reduced costs in terms of cutting down research time, marketing and raw material development technology. Further, it is a much simpler way to raise capital to grow a business as it comes with the advantage of not losing any portion of one's company or equity.

An alliance is considered effective when it is done with a financially healthy company in all ramifications, including assets, technological know-how as well as being able to locate a company that is also in alliance with other companies. In addition, there is the advantage of diversified strength in discovering a partner that is experienced and understands the rudiments of succeeding in strategic alliances.

Keeping Overheads low

It is vey important to ensure that overhead expenses are kept at a barest minimum. Consequently, costs which do not directly contribute to a project or marketing effort should be kept as low as possible. Similarly, expenses on rent of office, motor vehicle, stationery, etc. should be controlled. In addition, the need for a secretary may be done away with at the beginning of a consulting practice, while regarding the issue of an office; one could work from his home and cut out unnecessary expenses.

Further, to control the cost of telephone without a secretary, a consultant may consider using a voice mail or telephone answering service which enables clients to drop a message whenever he is not available. Care must however be taken to ensure that he get's back to the client's at the earliest time possible. Nevertheless, some clients will not leave a message on an answering machine. In such instances a consultant should ensure that the message on the answering machine is carefully worded to encourage callers to drop a message.

Signs Indicating the Need for the Services of a Consultant

The need for a consultant's services starts when a business realizes the need for one. In order words when it becomes pertinent to seek for outsider help to promote or grow the business from where it now is to where it ought to be.

Further, the US small business Administration (SBA), estimates that about 50% of small business outfits die within their first year of existence while on the other hand 95% of businesses fail within their first five (5) years of existence. Following signs make apparent ⌐he need for a consultant.

i.   Lack of properly written or documented business plan

A business plan is a document that spells out the direction that a business is to take in order to achieve its set goals and objective for coming into existence. This plans sets out the structure of the business, the mode of raising capital etc. including a detailed listing and analysis of risks and uncertainties. A lack of a properly written business plan therefore, is an invitation to chaos and a lack of a well-articulated set of objectives and targets to be achieved by the business. The business plan in a nutshell should explain the what, why, when and how of a project.

ii.   Rising increases in service cost

When the cost of service begins to increase without reasonable explanations over a period it may be wise to call in cost consultants to help look into the reasons or causes of these increases because an understanding of the cause of the unusual rise in prices could lead tc a permanent solution. Generally, the cost of a product or service may rise as a result of rises in cost of raw materials, transportation, packaging, fuel and energy costs etc.

iii. Low morale and overworking of staff

There is no substitute to a highly motivated workforce contented with what they do and thereby see the organization as their own. Motivaticn for staff of an organization come in several packages in the condʲtions of employments which are improved upon over time such as increases in the pay and salaries and overtime claims of workers, retirement benefits etc. for others, the environment they work in could be a source of motivation as well as the kind of caring leadership that is exuded by the company. Where morale is low indicating a lack of adequate incentives, a consultant may be required to show and provide workable solutions to help increase the morale of the workers thereby increasing production.

iv.   Consistent deficiency in supply

When there is a continual pattern of insufficient supply of the necessary input materials required for products and services then, the services of a consultant may be required to provide new insights and diagnoses of the causes and solutions to help stem the tide as well as seek out ways of getting more supplies from other sources.

v.   Lack of information about competitors

Competitors are those that strive for the same markets for clients like us hence the need to be constantly abreast of developments in the industry as well as the techniques and new ways being used by them to provide products and services thereby attracting new clients to patronize their companies. Again, a company needs to ask itself whether it is engaging in enough research and development of its products or service, as well as engaging in marketing and creating awareness to ensure that they retain client loyalty.

vi.   Mis-management

Mis-management is often a cause of business failure with big and well established companies. The demise of

ENRON and other corporate giants can be traced to mis-management by not playing according to the rules. Other forms of mis-management are in the areas of corporate frauds and embezzlement of company resources by employees placed in charge of the business.

Also worthy of note is the recent global financial crisis that has affected virtually all facets of the economies of various countries, particularly, the economic meltdown has touched the housing and mortgage, banking, stock and capital markets, manufacturing, especially the automotive industries and has seen companies declaring losses while others have been declared bankrupt.

Consequently, many governments, the US, Great Britain, the EU countries and others like Nigeria have embarked on stricter measures of financial control and surveillance over the business and financial sectors while some of these countries have also aided with bail out packages to help them survive the crises.

vii.   Lack of candor

Candor is the ability to be honest about situations as they affect a business. With candor a company cannot go wrong. But what is candor? It is simply the ability to tell it as it is. It is the ability to call a spade a spade no matter whose ox is gored. When candor is in place management and employees alike have the best interest of the company or organization at heart. No one is afraid to bring up an observation which could save the company from wasteful-ness, over expenditure on things that may not be beneficial in terms of cost and savings with the fear of being repri-manded by superiors or being held responsible for bringing up ideas for business that turns out to be a failure. Candor really sets everyone free to be able to think of or suggest new and better ways of doing things to beat the competition and for everyone in the company to have the 'our company' feeling.

viii. Lack of drive or interest

For a business to grow the owner(s) and management must show a lot of interest in how well it is working out. They must literally think, talk, dream and envision successful outcomes for the business. A moderate to a high drive is thus recommended to succeed.

ix.   Lack of sufficient capital

A lack of or insufficiency of capital required for a business idea is one of the main causes of business failure. Capital is required to start a business. Capital is the financial and monetary contribution of the owners of a business. Insufficient capital prevents an entrepreneur from having a feeling of pride at having created something new or re-directing and re-engineering a newly purchased business outfit or franchise with a potential for growth for the simple reason that its needs capital to put in place basic requirements to take off and grow. Capital is also required for expanding the base of a business and the level of its operations and diversification of portfolios.

x.   Lack of clear cut goals and objectives

Every business should have goals that it desires to achieve. These goals should be made a part of its mission statement. To be without a distinctive goal is to be like a sheep without a shepherd, to be without a goal is to be lost, without direction, without a purpose. Goals, mission statements, objectives all help to crystallize thinking by giving direction to a business plan and helping it get the business aspirations fulfilled.

xi.   Inadequate accounting records

Newly established companies often fail because of a lack of knowledge of how to keep proper records of accounts which are important for knowing the state of finances of a business.

xii.   Lack of co-ordination of all parts of a business

Effective co-ordination of all parts of a business is a given. Inability to ensure that all the component parts are adequately catered for holistically lead to distorted growth patterns which may not augur well for the business.

xiii. Lack of client satisfaction

A satisfied client is the best publicity there can be for a business. It is therefore expedient to ensure that clients are getting the best value for their money using a company's services.

xiv.   Inadequate market research to determine need or niche

Very often many go into business without carrying out enough research into the industry they propose to do business in. As a result, they are unable to determine what their target market should be and what needs there are to be met which consequently produces negative results for their businesses.

xv.   Overdrawing capital for personal use

Too often a business goes down because the owner fails to differentiate between company's finances and personal finances. In a sole proprietorship it is usually very difficult to separate the man from the business and therefore the finances of the business. The same might also be said for a partnership where the members in line with their agreement can draw money from capital. Now you and I know that there is every tendency to withdraw money from business working capital to solve pressing or personal problems with the intention of paying back at a later date but depending on how things turn out, moneys so borrowed end up not been completely refunded most of the time.

xvi.   Inefficiency in inventory management

A business may fail if it does not know how to keep proper records of its inventory. Consequently, when it fails to keep a track on its inventory, it will not know what it has in stock or may not be aware of the product being pilfered by its employees nor will it be abreast of the state of its inventory of product to determine its economic order quantity EOQ, its safety stock, or whether it has reached re-order level (ROL).

xvii. Too much investment on fixed assets

Too much money tied up on fixed assets freezes funds that are needed as working capital for a business which may cause it to fail because a proper balance is required. Consequently, a proper balance releases more funds for executing other pressing projects, commitments and obligations of an organization.

xviii. Choice of name of a business

What is in a name? You may ask. But names really do affect how a business is perceived. As a general rule, it is preferable to have a name other than one's own name in running a business especially if it not yet a household name. The names of some corporations are synonymous to quality whenever they are mentioned. Consequently the business name should reflect or have a bearing on what it does so that at a glance its mission is apparent from the onset.

xix. High Overhead

Overhead are business expenses and are the costs of carrying on a business in order to achieve a profit. Examples of overheads include administrative costs such as salaries and wages, production costs such as fuel and lubricant for company machinery, fixed costs such as rents etc. When overhead is high, it becomes extremely difficult for a company to make a profit or breakeven.

xx.   Low Revenue

Just as it is difficult to make a profit when overheads are high, it is also practically problematic for a company when its revenue from products or services are low possibly due to a lack of patronage from its target market-its desired clients. A company needs to take appropriate steps such as aggressive marketing and similar strategies to shore up sales and to enable it overcome this challenge.

Further, when sales targets are not been met and the company is seeking strategies for increcsing its sales, it may call in the relevant consulting agency to help it overcome or find new markets for products and services or to suggest other strategies it can adopt to help solve its dwindling sales problems.

xxi. Poor Business Skills

Poor business skills may stem out of a lack of the necessary technology and how to go about acquiring the right technology needed to propel the business from where it presently is to where it ought to be headed. Technology therefore, is that tool that enables a company to compete in an industry or global market.

xxii. Fresh ideas

When new ideas are needed in an organization to help it turn around the challenging situation it is being faced with, a consultant's services may be required to help it overcome whatever problems it is having. This helps to inject new perspectives to the situation thereby solving the problems being encountered by the client in his business.

xxiii. Personnel

There are occasions when a company decides to recruit new employees for its business. They may decide to do this through consulting agencies who are experts in searching for the appropriate executives to fill vacancies in the organization for a fee. In addition, when the company obtains a large contract say, from government, it may not have enough personnel to carry out the terms of the contract and at the same time do its normal business or to carry out other projects; in this case, it may decide to turn to a recruitment agency to assist in providing the necessary man power for a specified period or duration of the contract.

xxiv. The need to find new sources of Capital

Companies frequently need an injection of funds to enable them continue to deliver products and services to consumers. While, the problem of capital is usually associated with small businesses just starting out, big or established companies also require funds to help them expand their operations. Consequently, a consultant's skills for raising capital from various sources not immediately known or available to the client would be in high demand.

xxv. The need to keep abreast of government regulations as they affect a business

Governments very often make new policy statements which are expected to impact in one way or another on businesses, some of these pronouncements may mean that companies should take the necessary steps to understand the implications for their businesses which may therefore require the services of someone versed in the interpretation of government circulars and pronouncements on safety standards, age discrimination, equal employment opportunities etc.

xxvi. The need to improve efficiency

The situation often arise that the problem with a company's overall performance is basically due to inefficiencies or lapses in production, operations and general management. A consultant's role in such a situation when called upon will be to find the causes of these inefficiencies and to proffer necessary solutions to the results of their findings. Examples of inefficiencies can be found in such areas as delays, slippages, low productivity etc.

xxvii.   The need for training & capacity building

Consultants very often conduct training and capacity building for various organizations to help sharpen and update the skills and competence of employees of these organizations. Areas of training usually cover leadership, software programming needs, organizational and planning skills etc.

xxviii.   The problem of company politics

Very often an organization may desire to get certain things done but due to peculiar internal politicking, whereby members of staff are divided along different lines, many brilliant ideas for promoting and seeking or entering new markets never see the light of the day, the management may decide to instead make use of the services of a consulting firm in order to achieve objectivity since they are likely to be impartial in their approach.

xxix. The need for computers and IT

Computers and information technology needs of a business may require the services of a consulting firm to help in recommending and putting in place the appropriate systems for the organization.

xxx. The need to restore a system

In cases where companies are failing or going bankrupt, experienced consultants may be called upon to provide a turnaround for them. Some of these consultants may be required to head failing companies in order to carry out the necessary surgeries as it were until such a time that the companies recover or show signs of recovery.

Chapter 2
The Legal Structure of a Business

To commence on a sound footing a business is expected to meet all the requirements of the Revenue and Customs Authorities of the country it does business in by having the right legal structure as this will determine:

i.   The tax liabilities and national or social security of the business;
ii.   The accounting records that the business is required to keep;
iii. The financial liability of the business in the event of winding up or being wound up;
iv.   The mode of raising capital;
v.   How the organization's management makes decisions about the business.

Although various structures exist in law, we shall however discuss some of the more pertinent and commonly adopted ones.

a.   The Sole proprietorship;
b.   The Partnership;
c.   The Corporation.

The Sole Proprietorship

The sole proprietorship is the easiest form of legal structure to set up as it a business structure for a company owned by a single person. To establish a sole proprietorship, you only need to obtain the necessary licenses that are required in your local area. The sole proprietorship is used for many types of small businesses.

Advantages

1. Easy and quick to form- there are fewer formalities and legal requirements, the ease and speed of formation makes it possible to fulfill all the requirements within a short period and at a reasonable cost.

2. Reduced expense- the sole proprietorship does not usually require the expertise of an Attorney or Accountant and as such can be set up at a very minimal cost.

3. Total control-since there are no partners in the business, ownership and control therefore rests with the sole proprietor, as he has no boss technically speaking except of course his customers or clients. This makes the business responsive to changes in the market place.

4. Sole claim to profit- since ownership of the business rests with the sole proprietor; it follows that profits generated by the business will be his for the keeping.

Disadvantages

1. Unlimited liabilities- the sole proprietor bears the brunt and liabilities of his business in the event of failure. This puts the weight of claims by creditors on his personal assets as well as assets of his organization. One way of minimizing this risk is for management to ensure that it has procured the necessary insurance coverage on its assets.

2.   Lone ranger- the sole proprietor is alone in running his business and therefore has to depend on his skills, education, background, and capabilities. Even when he receives advice from friends, relatives or business acquaintances, the implementation and consequences remain his sole responsibility.

3.   Difficulty when unavoidably absent- the business may be closed to the public when the sole proprietor is unavoidably absent or even sick or on vacation. This can however be overcome by employing someone to look after the business while he is away or asking a friend, relative or business acquaintance to cover for him during his absence.

4.   Difficulty in raising finance- except a business has track records of successes; lenders are likely to be skeptical about giving loans to the firm or organization.

The Partnership

A partnership exists where two or more persons agree to run or establish a business by pooling their resources together and sharing the profits and losses that will eventually be generated by the business. Following are various forms of partnerships that may be adopted by intending partners.

i.   Dormant partner

This kind is also referred to as silent partners since he does not partake in the day-to—day running of the business but contributes financially to it.

ii.   Active partner

This kind is involved in the day-to-day activities of the business as well as contributing financially to it. The active partner may however draw a salary depending on the agreement reached by the partners.

iii.   General

This kind is personally liable in the event of any unpaid business debt or other obligations.

iv.   Limited

A limited partner is only liable to the amount already invested in the business by him.

v.   Limited liability partner

Here, the partners enjoy limited liability and is common among professionals such as accountants and attorneys since they are not allowed to use corporations to limit their liabilities. Limited liability partnerships offer the advantage of favorable tax liabilities enjoyed by partnerships as well as the liability protections of a corporation.

A partnership differs from a sole proprietorship in the following ways:

a.   Co-ownership of the assets of the business;
b.   Mutual agency;
c.   Limited life of the partnership;
d.   Unlimited liability of at least one of the partners;
e.   Sharing of business profits;
f.   Sharing of managerial responsibilities.

Partnership agreements generally speaking cover the following areas:

i.   Absence and disability;
ii.   Arbitration;
iii.   Authority of individual partners in the conduct of the business;
iv.   Character of the partners, whether active, dormant, etc;
v.   Dissolution of the partnership, if and when necessary;
vi.   Division of profits and losses;
vii.   Salary and amounts a partner can withdraw at any particular time during the growth of the business;
viii. Contributions by each of the partners on commencement and afterwards, during the growth of the business;
viii. Managerial assignments within and outside the firm;
ix.   Duration of the agreement;
xi.   Handling of expenditures by partners;
xii.   Method of accounting and book keeping;
xiii. Assessment of performance of partners;
xiv.   Release of debts;
xv.   Name, purpose, and place of partnership;
xvi.   Required and prohibited acts;
xvii. Rights of continuing partners;
xviii. Sale of partnership interest;
xix.   Settlement of disputes;
xx.   Separate debts.

Advantages
i.   Assistance in decision making

When there is a need to seek counsel from another; he receives insight for solving and resolving a problem. A partnership has this added advantage when compared with the sole proprietorship.

ii.   Easy and quick to form

Like the sole proprietorship a partnership is also easy to form.

iii.   Access to additional capital

As a result of the pooling of resources by partners, additional funds are available to them.

iv.   Vacation and sickness stability

One partner is able to cover for the other whenever he or she is unavailable or temporarily indisposed.

Disadvantages
i.   Difficulty in obtaining capital

Because partnerships are viewed as less stable when compared with corporations, they are considered more risky investments in terms of granting of loans or capital to them.

ii.   Liability for the actions of partners

Each partner is bound by the actions or inactions of the others.

iii.   Potential organizational disputes

Disagreements are normal in every human relation-ship however; if they are not well handled they could lead to negative consequences. Likewise partnerships are not spared from this.

The Corporation

A corporation is a legal entity that is separate and distinct from its owners. It is not usually a simple organization in the sense that its structure can be somewhat complicated. In forming a corporation the services of an attorney may be required especially with regards to the requirements of the laws of a country, or state.

Advantages
i.   Additional human resources

This is possible because of the requirement of a board of directors since they are qualified to offer direction to a company especially in periods of crisis or difficulty.

ii.   Credibility to clients in industry

This advantage may be attributed to its long-term structure although this may become a minor advantage because a company's reputation is a function of its credibility.

iii.   Relative ease in obtaining capital

Because of its permanent legal structure and going concern nature, lenders are more willing to make loans to them. Some banks however, require smaller corporations to personally co-sign loans.

iv.   Limited liability

A corporation as a separate legal entity is recognized as a person in law, consequently its owners are only liable to the amounts of investments held by them.

Disadvantages

i.   Income taxes

Affect corporations negatively as a result of the inci-
dences of double taxation.

ii.   Board of directors

The law to have a board of directors and to also comply with additional local, state, and federal government
laws requires reduced control since it is a corporation; its
control abilities are therefore greatly reduced.

iii.   Inability to take losses as deductions

Sole proprietorships and partnerships may be able to
take losses as deductions, unlike corporations that are only
allowed to carry forward their losses. However, this seeming
disadvantage can be overcome by the formation of a special type of corporation-the S-corporation.

iv.   Additional paperwork and government regulations

A lot of work may be involved when companies are
being formed as a result of the paper work required and
also in complying with government regulations.

v.   Expensive to form

This is due to its structure and the requirement of the
services of an attorney.

The S Corporation

The S corporation is mainly targeted at small companies
to enable them benefit from having their incomes taxed to

the shareholder like a partnership. This has the advantage of avoiding an occurrence of double taxation, thereby giving the investor the advantage of incorporating without the taxation disadvantage.

The following requirements must be fulfilled in order to qualify as an S corporation. These are:

1. There must be a maximum of ten shareholders who should be individuals or estates;
2. All shareholders are required to be resident especially where they are aliens;
3. Only one class of outstanding shares or stocks is permissible;
4. All shareholders must consent to the election of S corporation treatment;
5. Specific portions of the receipts of the corporation must come from actual business activities rather than passive investments.

Chapter 3
Finding Solutions to Problems in a Professional Way

People become consultants when they use their skills and competences in such a way that they groom and sharpen their knowledge to enable them solve the problems or challenges of others. When there is c need for advice and counselling someone who is able to provide workable and effective solutions is the one who will be sought after by people. The individual skilled in some area of endeavour, say counselling, sports , managing people etc. may want to consider making this a consulting opportunity by horning and sharpening his skills in such a way as to be useful to others that may need his services.

What is consulting?

Consulting is the art of helping others solve their problems in a professional way. It has been estimated that the consulting industry is worth over a hundred billion ($100 billion dollars) as a result of technological advances such as the Internet with all its advantages. A consultant therefore, is that person who has skills and competence useful to others in such a way that they actually seek him out to help them find solutions to challenges in their various areas of endeavour based on his area of specialization for a fee.

A Skill is the ability, coming from one's knowledge, practice, aptitude etc. to do something well, while competence is the quality of being competent; adequacy; possession of required skill, knowledge, qualification, or capacity.

Further, although it is advisable to have an advanced degree to be a consultant, it is however not a mandatory requirement even though the orientation of a consultant is obviously a professional one. What is required of a consultant is that he should have the necessary experience, qualifications, and skill to undertake or carry out the task that an individual or company wants executed.

Who is a Management Consultant?

Individuals who desire to work for already established consulting firms rather than working for themselves go into what is known as management consultancy which is primarily concerned with initiating and implementing technological and behavioural changes. Management consultants are engaged to provide wider additional expertise than is available within a single organization. In addition, they provide objective appraisals where it is thought that the advice of an expert's outsider to see the broader picture and to recognise the long-term requirements as well as to provide additional assistance where there is a temporary increase in management workload, especially coping with a major change or new development in a specified area of management responsibility is necessary.

Typically those going into management consulting are 25-35 as new entrants tend to fall into this age group. This age range is by no means sacrosanct as younger people with MBA degrees and the requisite knowledge and desire to become consultants go in as prospective consultants. However, older entrants may be required to bring along with them at least 3 three years management experience.

Independent consulting

Independent consulting is a situation where someone or a group of people who have skills and services to offer clients undertake the task of providing useful advice of a professional nature to those in need of them for a fee. This may be in the form of helping them re-organize their lives and business, among others.

Qualities of a consultant

i.   Management skills

Management means getting things done through other people. This is a very important skill as it helps the consultant get to terms with running his consulting practice.

ii.   Ability to get along with your client

This involves coming to the level of the client in a way that he feels comfortable and having confidence in what the consultant says.

iii.   Ability to identify a problem and solve it

A good and competent consultant should be able to diagnose the problems being faced by his client in order to provide workable solutions.

iv.   Requisite skill & expertise required to pull off a job

At all times he must continue to horn and update his skills and expertise in order to remain relevant. He should ensure that he accepts only the jobs that he knows and feels confident to pull off.

v.   Ability to communicate effectively

The ability to communicate is one of the most pertinent skills of a good consultant as he will need this singular skill all through his consulting practice. In addition, he should be armed with appropriate analytical skills and should also be able to work under pressure so as to meet any deadline.

vi.   Must have marketing and selling skills

Marketing is the sum total of activities involved in the transfer of products and services from the producer or seller to the consumer or buyer, including advertising, shipping, storing, and selling. A consultant is engaged in selling an intangible service and should therefore sharpen this skill because he needs to be a good marketer of the products or services of his consulting practice.

Types of consulting firms

a.   Finance and Accounting firms;

Finance and accounting firms include financial, management and cost accounting as well as taxation and investment services.

b.   Management firms

These include firms dealing with general management and organizational strategy etc.

c.   Functionally specialized firms

Functionally specialized firms concentrate on many areas such as telecommunication and executive search or recruitment.

d.   Public sector firms

These firms deal mainly with government and its agencies at all levels, i.e. local, state and national levels as well as with non-profit organizations.

e.   Industry specific firms & the so called think tank

Firms that consult exclusively for particular clients who may be few in number are called industry specific or think tank firms. Examples include Aviation consulting firms or firms that consult for the armed forces and other specialised utility institutions.

f.   Specialty firms outside of business

These are firms that look outside their primary areas or target markets into areas such as the provision of fashion, health, etiquettes, tourism and other similar services.

g.   Regional and local firms

Regional and local firms make a great proportion of their earnings from a particular area or environment such as in a state, local government or region.

h.   Sole practitioners

A sole practitioner is more or less a one man consulting business frequently utilized by new entrants to the consulting business and also by consulting businesses with between two to ten employees.

Scope of consulting

a)   General management- covering organizational strategy and management of a company or organization.

b)   Manufacturing- dealing with facilities manage-
     ment and production control.

c)   Personnel- involves the development of manage-
     ment of employee benefits and pensions, training,
     recruitment, selection of employee benefits etc.

d)   Marketing- dealing with issues of development of
     distribution channels, promotion, pricing, as well
     as new service development.

e)   Finance and accounting-consists of financial, cost
     and management accounting services as well as
     taxation and allied services

f)   Procurement and purchasing- dealing with the
     acquisition of products and/or services at the best
     possible cost of ownership, in the right quantity
     and quality, at the right time, in the right place
     and from the right source for the direct benefit or
     use of corporations or individuals, generally with
     the aid of a contract.

g)   Research and development- refers to creative
     work undertaken on a systematic basis in order to
     increase the stock of knowledge, including knowl-
     edge of man, culture and society, and the use of
     this stock of knowledge to devise new applica-
     tions.

h)   Packaging- is the act, process, industry, art, or
     style of packing or the manner in which some-
     thing, such as a proposal or service, or someone,
     such as a candidate or author, is presented to the
     public.

i)   Administration- is the act or process of administering, especially the management of a government or large institution.

j)   International operations- involve Joint ventures, import, export, tariffs, and licensing etc.

k)   Specialized services-include telecommunications, executive recruitment and search services.

Requirement for succeeding in consulting

i.   Planning- the ability to make conscious efforts at preparing a template for an organization by helping it have direction, goals and objectives and focus etc.

ii.   Searching out and basing decisions on facts as opposed to making assumptions.

iii. Being as simple as possible in everything one does.

iv.   Having a high self concept by being confident and coming across as a success.

v.   Putting the interest of the client's first and demonstrating commitment and reliability.

vi.   Seeking out opportunities to adequately, relevantly and effectively promote what one does.

vii. Keeping in touch with one's clients thereby making them feel special.

viii. Letting the client understand the intricacies of the assignment by getting them involved and also finding out from them through referrals and evaluations what they think of the work.

ix. Constantly evaluating and analysing the business to know how it is performing.

How to Solve any Problem

Problems are the challenges that we encounter in our daily lives that require solutions to them. Problem solving is therefore a series of mental activity targeted at solving or surmounting a challenge or difficulty. A problem when solved helps one graduate from one level of problem solving to the other since life is never free from problems. Indeed, as long one lives problems are bound to occur. This is a fact that should be embraced to gain insight and become confident that every problem can be solved as the seed or solution to any problem is often contained in the problem itself.

In order to solve problems critical decisions will be made among competing options in terms of the best possible course of action to take in solving or resolving issues. Decisions are simply judgements taken among possible choices or options for solving the problems. Effective decision making involves managers or supervisors engaging themselves and their mental faculties in the process of identification, assessment, choice, planning, execution and follow- up. Basically, many managers solve problems differently using styles that are unique mixed with tested decision making models. These managers employ rational or intuitive thought processes to solve or reach a decision.

Rational thinking consists of the following steps in reaching a decision.

i.   Use of knowledge, skills and experience;

ii.   Application of logic to reaching a conclusion;

iii.   Analyses of issues to get an appropriate understanding of the problem.

Intuitive thinking on the other hand consists of employing:

i.   Hunches to reach conclusions,

ii.   Emotions and sensitivity to reach a decision,

iii.   Imaginative processes to create new ideas.

In addition to the above, decision makers often use what is known as the basic model in making decisions. The basic model is a series of steps calibrated into 9 stages which give a reasonable guide for reaching decisions quickly while allowing the user to start and end at any point of the rung he feels confident that the problem has been resolved. This means that there are no hard and fast rules as the decision maker is allowed to recycle through the stages as he deems fit according to the level of new information and situation that become evident at every stage. This he does when:

i.   He recognises the problem field

To recognise a problem field, one necessarily has to look at the whole gamut of issues surrounding the problem at hand which leads one to make concerted efforts at finding out what the problem really is. By so doing, the problem rather than the symptoms of the problem itself is treated.

ii.   Identifies the problem

To identify a problem, an individual must examine the circumstance that surrounds the problems. In essence, he should collect, analyse and interpret the facts at his disposal. Thus, the decision maker is advised to concentrate on the most relevant and essential information in solving the problem and quickly reaching a decision.

iii.   Specifies the problems

This stage is time and cost consuming and is the stage at which only essential information is sought for specific problems by defining the facts through asking relevant questions such as who, what, how and how often the problem occurs.

iv.   Diagnoses the problem

A diagnosis is the real key to decision making and is a very pertinent stage that aims at searching for the cause of the problem through the use of the scientific method. When the causes of a problem are known what is left would be to search for appropriate solutions that will help solve them.

v.   Sets objectives

When problems are identified the next thing to do is to seek solutions or ways to neutralize the causes and by implication the problems themselves.

vi.   Generates alternative plans

This stage involves analysing as many options or alternatives that are likely to help solve the problem and to select the best possible option. This however, entails taking the following steps and actions:

a)   Inactivity or doing nothing about the situation until it becomes evidently clear that the steps being taken to resolve issues would likely lead to the best outcome.

b)   Brainstorming with colleagues and friends on the problem at hand with a view to having more inputs that will help unlock insights to solving the problem at hand.

c)   Applying the power of the sub-conscious as the mind also has intuitive powers to solve any problem when it is given the chance to do so.

vii.   Evaluates alternative plans

Evaluating alternative plans involve looking at the pros and cons of using the alternative. In this regards the advantages and disadvantages of each possible alternative as well as the opportunity cost of the alternative forgone.

viii. Makes the decision

Having selected the best alternative or option, the next step is to proceed to making the decision. The critical issue here is judgement and objectivity to be able to make the best possible decision. To decide is to:

a)   Take action;
b)   To take risks;
c)   Court failure.

Consequently, individuals and managers are duty bound to select the most appropriate solution to a problem; one that gives the greatest promise of maximum returns to all parties.

ix.   Sets standards and controls for actions

This entails detailing a course of action for plans, objectives, policies etc. which is necessary as decisions in themselves are nothing until they have been implemented and backed with well programmed actions.

Chapter 4
Financing your Consulting Business

For many people with genuine interest in starting their own consulting practice, getting the funds to start or expand can be a very thorny issue. However, one could start by putting away some amount of money in savings as no one will believe in the project if one has not taken the first step to show a burning desire to succeed and the ability to attract the resources required in pulling off the project. However, there is no prescribed way to start a consulting business other than to comply with al legal requirements in a country or intended place of business.

Factors to Consider in Choosing a Means of Finance

a. Cost- this is important in that the cost of a product or finance is cardinal to knowing whether it will be a viable option among other sources of raising finance for a project. If the associated cost of choosing a means of finance is high it may defeat the purpose for which it was sought for in the first place. Consequently, there is a need to ponder over this before committing the organizations assets to any source of finance.
b. Duration- the duration of a project can help determine the source of finance that should be employed by an organization. Short term projects should seek short term financing while long term projects should make use of long term funds.

c.   Term structure of interest rates- refers to the relation-
      ship between bonds of different terms. When interest
      rates are plotted against their terms, this is called the
      yield curve. It is a common belief that the shape of the
      yield curve reflects the markets future expectations for
      interest rates and provides the necessary conditions for
      monetary policy.
d.   Gearing- is the ratio of debt to equity (company's long
      term funds). A high gearing is generally considered
      very speculative as the higher the gearing, the greater
      the proportion of cheap debt/finance and the higher
      the risk to shareholders.
e.   Accessibility- it is a known fact that not all companies
      have access to all sources of funding. Particularly, small
      companies are more likely to encounter problems in
      raising equity and long term debt finance.

Main Ways of Financing a Business

Typically, a business may be financed in two ways; internal or external sources.

1.   Internal Sources

a.   Personal Savings

Personal savings are those savings that overtime have
been set aside not necessarily because there is a deliberate plan for the money saved, but a habit formed in pru-
dent management of resources at ones disposal and kept
aside for a 'rainy day'. Forming a habit of saving money is
something that is encouraged because one never know's
when it will come in useful.

However, as an aspiring consultant this is not to say
that you should not save for a purpose, on the contrary if

you desire to go into business at some time in the future, then you are advised to start saving without delay because the amount of capital required to start a business in these days of information technology is not really as colossal as you may suppose. The only other ingredient that may be required is your willingness to start small and grow your business to the desired level through tenacity of purpose, determination and commitment to succeed in what you do.

b.   Retained Earnings

Retained earnings are profits ploughed back into a business by the owners to help ensure its growth and continuity. Retained earnings may be used to improve the business by providing readily available funds to help it function well. These profits are used to purchase additional machineries, computers etc. which is also a way of saving for periods of financial difficulties.

c.   Working Capital

Working capital is the fund required to keep a business going from day to day. It includes funds utilized for the payment of rents, rates, stationery, energy & electricity bills, payment for supplies etc. it is expressed as the difference between current assets and current liabilities.

d.   Disposal of Assets

Assets are those things that are owned by a company or business. They include items such as landed properties, furniture's and fittings, motor vehicles etc. A company may wish to sell off some of its assets in order to generate more funds for the business; the proceeds from sales can therefore be regarded as an internal source of capital for the business. Further, Assets like, land, properties, motor vehicles etc. that are lying dormant and not being utilized can be channeled into wealth creation avenues like rents of the properties, and cultivation of the land for agricultural purposes thereby generating revenue by providing additional sources of income for the business.

e.   Hobby, Interest, Talent

Hobbies that one is good at provide indications of possible business opportunities to be derived from an exploration of their potentials. Hobbies provide great possibilities for starting a business that could become a big corporation someday. Many people have turned their hobbies into money making machines as a result of seeing opportunities that are often never considered by others.

There are skills and expertise that people require like house and interior decorations, being able to make people laugh (comedy), being a master of ceremony, technical abilities such as being able to fix things with ease and which may be keyed into by the individual who really wishes to make tangible gains out of them. Hobbies and skills when properly harnessed enable you experiment with your hands and to also think deeply with a questioning mind on those things that you seem to do well.

f.   Training and Apprenticeship

Someone who has undergone pupilage or tutelage in a master apprentice or master servant relationship, more often than not starts a business. Under this method the student acquires business experience by understudying his boss and master while carrying out his instructions the student learns the ropes of the business and after the agreed numbers of years have elapsed he is freed and enabled with capital and other logistical supports by his master to start his own business.

g.   Inheritance

Coming into an inheritance is another way to start a business. An inheritance immediately makes available to the inheritor a measure of money or money's worth which if not properly utilized could fritter away the original owners' years of labor and toil in a very short space of time. It is therefore important and wise to immediately consider how to grow the money or its worth in ones possession by ensuring it is wisely invested.

2.   External Sources

a.   Equity

Equity is also referred to as ordinary shares. As owners of a company, they have a right to profit after other obligations of companies have been considered. Ordinary shareholders have a right to vote at the general meetings of a company. The right to vote means they can decide the fate of a company in terms of the appointment of auditors, directors, change the memorardum or constitution of the company, as well as decide whether the amount of dividend declared by the company is acceptable to them or not. Depending on the outcome of their decisions they may accept or reject the dividend declared by the company. Ordinary shares are risky in the sense that there is no guarantee as to whether they will receive a dividend or not in a particular year since dividend declaration is tied to the performance of the company.

Thus, it is the ordinary shares that are quoted on the stock exchange (a second hand market). This class of shares helps to determine the market capitalization of a firm. Market capitalization is the number of ordinary shares owned by a company on the stock exchange multiplied by the price of the shares. For example suppose company A, has 5,000 ordinary shares with a market price of 50cents per share, then the market capitalization of company A, will be 5,000 x 50 cents which equals $2,500.

Further, ordinary shares can either be sold at nominal or face value, which is the value on the share certificate or at market value, which is the price at which it is being sold on the stock exchange. In essence, shares can either be traded off at par or at a premium. Shares sold at par means that they have been sold at the face value of the shares. A share at a premium means that the shares have been sold for more than their face value.

b.   Debt (Preference Shares)

Preference shares have a right to be paid their dividend regardless of the situation of a company whether it is making profits or not. In the event the company has not made sufficient profit to enable payment of preference shares, the amount outstanding will be carried over to the next dividend that will be declared especially if it is a cumulative preference share. It is called a preferences share because it has a first claim to profit before the ordinary shares.

c.   Business Angels

These are individuals with the funds to assist a business with capital when approached with a meaningful and viable proposal. Angel financing is now a very popular way of obtaining the much needed capital to fund a project. Like all loans they come with conditions as agreed between these angels and those in need of finance for their business.

d.   Loans from Friends, Relations and Family

Loans from family and friends provide a veritable means of raising funds or capital for a business. As with all loans the viability of the business must first be communicated to these category of people and if they are convinced, they may offer necessary assistance without the kind of strings that are usually associated with lcans obtained from banks and other sources as family and fr ends look upon the success of someone going into business as perscnally theirs and would feel very proud if the business succeeds.

e.   Loans from Bank

A loan is something lent for temporary use or a sum of money lent at an interest. It is a very important source of raising capital for a business. Loans given for the purpose of raising finance for a business, vary depending on the circumstances of the borrower as the conditions for granting a loan usually depends on the amount of a loan, the amount of the interest, the repayment date, the qualification of the recipient of the loan that encbles him or her to receive the loan, the credit analysis, and the number of lenders used to achieve the desired loan.

Chapter 5
Effective Research on Consulting Projects

Research is an academic response to problems of any kind. Helmstadter defines it as "the activity of solving problems which lead to a new knowledge using methods of enquiry which are currently acceptable by researchers in the field". For man, the importance of research cannot be adequately expressed because it is a crucial tool for the advancement of knowledge, for promoting progress and for enabling man to relate more effectively with the environment in order to resolve conficts. Aver speaks of research as something that is essentially based on enquiry having procedures that include observation of available facts, relating to a particular problem followed by the formation of hypothesis or theoretical solutions, used for practical testing of the experiment or of the theory to obtain evidence, for a conclusion, or generalisation.

Further, methodology is the basic conceptual framework on which the whole research is based. A research design should combine relevance to the research purpose.

Methods of Data Collection

The collection of data requires mastering certain basic skills and involves obtaining relevant information regarding the major hypothesis for the purpose of demonstrating whether or not they are true. Basically, there are two sources of data collection, namely:

i.   Primary sources

Primary data refer to information being collected for the first time through any of the following methods.

a.   Interview

Interviews are acts of verbal communications for the purpose of drawing or bringing out information. It is any conversational exchange whereby one person seeks information from another. The interview method is mainly used when the interviewer desires a reliable and valid data in the form of verbal responses. During the duration of the interview both parties usually behave as if they are of equal status.

Further, there are basically 4 types of interview, namely:

•   Structured

    This involves the use of rigidly standardised and formalised questions addressed to respondents. In structured interviews, responses are normally limited to simple alternatives or multiple choice questions in the form of Yes or No, or Good or Bad types. In addition, fixed response questions present information which can be classified and quantified such as when the respondents are children or illiterates, in which pictorial data collection method could be used. Pictorial data collection method involves the drawing of a graph or photograph instead of a written statement which is presented to the respondents. It needs to be said however, that this method of data collection can only be utilized where the visual characteristics are easily understood and can be distinguished especially

when the pictures are photographs of human be-
ings even though they are often difficult to stan-
dardise.

- Unstructured

  In this type of method of interviews, respondents
  are allowed to express themselves freely, since the
  questions are set in a flexible manner and the discussions could go beyond the initial question.

- Non- directive depth interview

  This kind of interview allows the respondent to talk
  freely and fully on any topic, which makes it easy
  to assess someone being interviewed more closely, in terms to the behaviour, motives and beliefs.

- Focused interview

  A focused interview is one that allows the respondent to talk freely and fully bu¯ required to comply
  with the specification of the questions in line with
  the directions of the interviewer.

Advantages of the Interview Method

    i.   There is no room for rapport which is neces-
sary to make the respondent feel at ease and
disposed to hearing and answering questions.

    ii.   Interviews allow probing and prodding into
the context and reasons for answers to the
question.

iii.   It is a flexible method that is applicable to different types of problems.

Disadvantages of the Interview Method

i.   Responses may be influenced by biases of the interviewer.

ii.   It consumes a lot of time.

iii. It is difficult to generalise from unstructured interviews.

b.   Questionnaires

The questionnaire method involves gathering specific data relating to identified problems through the use of questionnaires. It is made up of a list of questions relating to the aims of the study and the hypothesis to be verified which the respondent is expected to answer by writing in the response.

There are mainly three types of questionnaire designs, namely:

i.   Open ended questionnaires;
ii.   The fixed choice or confined questionnaires;
iii. The pictorial questionnaire.

Open ended questionnaires allow the respondents to answer in their own words. As a result, maximum information can be obtained and bias is eliminated. Open ended questions come in handy and Open ended questionnaires are especially useful in situations where there is difficulty in formulating positive alternatives. Three conditions need to be met before adequate responses can be given by a respondent.

i.   He must understand the questions clearly.
ii.   The required information must be provided by the right respondent.
iii. The respondent must be willing to provide the needed information.

Shortcomings of the Questionnaire Method

i.   The result achieved may contain elements of bias unless a random sample of the questionnaire is carried out.

ii.   The respondent may be influenced by other people who are not relevant to the study since the respondent is not under the control or supervision of the interviewer thereby producing a biased result.

iii. Questionnaires do not provide for extra information to be attached to it.

c.   Observation

The observation method is an important tool for primary data collection in any scientific research just as science begins with observation for its validity. It is used where the interview and questionnaire methods are not suitable. When properly conducted the observation method does the following.

i.   It captures the social context in which a person's behaviour occurs.

ii.   It captures the important events that affect social relations of the participants.

iii.   It determines what reality means from a world view and philosophy or outlook of the observed.

iv.   It identifies the frequency and occurrences in social life by comparing and contrasting data obtained in one study to those obtained in studies of other natural settings.

There are basically two types of observation methods and they are:

i.   The participant method observation method

Here actions are observed in their natural context.

ii.   The non- participant observation method.

Under this method, the actions of others are closely observed with the researcher not being a part of the group. This method has been criticized in some schools of thoughts while others have opined otherwise.

Advantages of observation methods

a)   Observation method is suitable where people are not willing to express themselves verbally.

b)   It enables the gathering of revealing and valuable information provided logical and un-biased approach to the observation is taken.

c)   Since this method allows a recording of behaviour in its natural setting, it can help behavioural studies in their natural occurrences.

Disadvantages of Observation Method

a) There is a difficulty in the standardisation of results due to the fact that some of the information obtained may not be quantifiable.

b) There could be biases in the information obtained.

c) The exercise may be time consuming considering the length of time it may take for its completion spanning weeks, months or years.

ii.   Secondary Data

Secondary data on the other hand refers to the information obtained from records of all kinds that have been written down. It is the first type of data to look for before making use of the primary sources which include such things as speeches, autobiographies, rhetorical records, newspaper accounts of events, general articles, magazines, court of various kinds etc. The data so obtained may either be internal or external.

• Internal Secondary Data Sources

Sources of these data comprise sales and accounting data, and internally generated research reports which are found within organizations where the research is being conducted.

• External Sources of Data

These play a very pertinent role n the gathering of information and include:

Publications of government agencies, e.g. Federal Office of Statistics (F.O.S), Federal Ministry of Information and Communication, etc;

Trade and Professional Associations, e.g. American Marketing Association, Association of National Accountants of Nigeria, American Institute of Certified Public Accountants, The Institute of Management Consultants etc.

Miscellaneous published Newspapers, dissertations, books and monographs, specialised published reports etc.

Advantages of Secondary Data Method

a)   Compared to primary data, it is less costly.

b)   It saves time.

c)   When it is difficult to obtain information from primary sources, secondary data comes in useful.

Disadvantages of Secondary Data

There are two major disadvantages of secondary data and they are:

i.   Inappropriate data;
ii.   Inaccurate data.

Secondary data has limitations compared to primary data. It is therefore very critical to choose the appropriate method in order to derive maximum benefit. As a consultant, you are therefore expected to have knowledge of the advantages and disadvantages of the methods you intend to use.

Chapter 6
Preparing and Making your Initial Interview a success

It is the responsibility of a consultant to ensure that he is appropriately dressed for the occasion as his client in all probability will hold a view that is rather suspicious of his level or degree competence to address the problem under review. It is therefore imperative that he carries himself in a professional and confident manner in terms of behaviour and comportment.

A simple rule is for you, the consultant; to dress like the client. This makes him feel comfortable with you as he is able to from the onset see an area where you are alike. Equally important is the need to maintain a professional attitude devoid of arrogance by being friendly and making him feel that he could entrust his prob ems to you.

In addition, you need to be on the same wavelength with your client through building rapport which may stem from your common interest, background or experience. This may involve mirroring and matching the tempo and voice of your client in terms of speech, breath, word usage, postures, and general body language or movements. The key to doing this successfully is to practice or rehearse and get the necessary feedback on how you have performed before the day of the interview. Self assessment is cardinal to a successful outcome.

Suggestions for Ensuring that the Essentials are captured during the initial Interview

To conduct a successful interview it is important to do the following

a.   Take notes during the interview

A tape recorder is not a recommended option because it makes your client feel less secure as he may be intimidated to think that what ever he says may later be used inappropriately by you. Ask questions to be sure that there is no mis-understanding and to find out all there is to know about the assignment. It is also necessary to request for items and tools that will aid performance of the job at hand. These items include your client's service brochures annual reports or other documents that are crucial for the successful performance of the assignment.

b.   Pay attention to your client

As a rule your client should be left to do the talking while you do the listening. This will ensure that all he has to say is exhausted during the first interview. Consequently, my advice is that you should avoid suggesting solutions to the problem from the onset even if they are apparent on the first interview as this may lead him to conclude that there may be no further need for engaging your services since the solution to his problem has already been identified and solved by you.

c.   Body language

When clients speak with their arms folded across their chest and avoiding eye contact with fist clenched and a wrinkled brow, such actions may suggest that they are non committal and are already threatened by the situation at hand and are not confident that the solution to the problem lies with you or put differently that you can solve the problem. It is best to refrain from pressing the issue further by allowing matters to rest and also adopting other approaches that make him appear forthcoming with the information required to deliver an effective service. The key is to play the role of a psychologist who studies his client for any revealing signs about what he has refused to reveal or is not saying verbally.

When a client begins to feel comfortable it will become apparent as his fist and demeanour or countenance and general comportment will begin to change and become rather friendly. Further, when he appears eager or excited at the solutions being proposed by you, this may indicate that he is willing to go ahead with the assignment and to do everything in his powers to see that the problem is eventually solved. But if on the other hand he appears to be in thought and is biting the edge of the pencil or pen, leans back with the hand at the back of the head, and strokes the chin, it indicates that he is listening and evaluating what is being proposed by you and trying to reach a decision on the engagement.

Basically facial expressions may be categorised into 10 or more types.

- Happy and contented,
- Surprised,
- Angry,

- Upset, disguised,
- Fearful,
- Upset,
- Bored, not interested,
- Tired, relieved, relaxed,
- Puzzled, not sure,
- Devious, sly.

It is the your responsibility as a consultant to attempt a summary of what has been said during the interview which should be read and confirmed with your client that they are actually as he or she has intended. You should also remember to avoid using words that appear to contradict those of your client rather you should employ words that are neither in agreement nor in dis-agreement with him. Use words such as "How interesting", "I see", "Really", "I understand".

Finally, end the interview by thanking and telling him that you are interested in helping to solve the problem when you observe that he may be willing to cede the assignment to you. Also inform your client how he will be billed. This is usually done for short and special assignments.

7 Problem Areas to Address

Following are critical areas that you should do well to pay attention to.

a.   The problem to be solved

Identify why your client has requested your presence or what you can do for him. It is not unusual to find that your client is reluctant to come clean with you since he does not yet know you well enough to reveal all his problems to you. You should endeavour to make your client feel at home

with you by comporting yourself appropriately and professionally thereby allaying his fears.

b.   What your client wants done

This involves determining the purpose of the engagement. That is, what does your client want you to do for him
e.g. product development, personnel recruitment or ratio-
nalisation, or reducing the rate of employee turnover or increasing sales etc.

c.   Specific areas that are off limit

Ask your client about areas that are highly toned and
which he may like to avoid. This is because all organizations
play certain levels of politics and not understanding this will
lead you to get involved in the internal quagmire that may
leave you worse off than when you first came even if you
eventually manage to solve the problem.

d.   Recognizing when the objective is met

Agree with your client on the criteria to determine that
what is being sought for has been achieved e.g. 10% sales
or turnover reduction. It is important to be specific about
what the targets are with your client before commencing
the assignment.

e.   The main point of contact

The main point of contact means someone with whom
you are to carry on the assignment. You should endeavour
to keep the phone number and name and title of this individual.

f.   Alternate contact person

In addition to the main contact, also request for an alternate contact as a back-up in the event that the main contact is indisposed to avoid wasting time. The number and title should be taken down as well.

g.   Level of influence of participants

You should also ensure that you know the people you are to be in touch with to avoid receiving inputs for the work that at the end of the day may have come from those who do not have the authority to offer such and which may lead your client to doubt your ability, which may impinge on your continuing as a client in future.

Chapter 7
Sharpening your Negotiating Skills

Negotiation is a very important part of any organization's relationship. It is engaged in order to produce an agreement between opposing parties. Negotiations take place in almost every area of our lives on a daily basis. For example, we negotiate with our spouses on who is better placed to do what, say; picking the children from school because one of us would be engaged in some other equally important schedule. It is a form of alternative dispute resolution mechanism often employed in settling parties in areas where no common agreement has been arrived at. Negotiations also take place in other scenarios like the settlement of labour disputes, discussions with suppliers, employees, partners and clients for the purpose of achieving goals that are beneficial and satisfying to all concerned parties.

Criteria for Negotiations

Eric Skopec and Laree Kielly give some useful insights on how to identify the type of Negotiation strategy to adopt under certain circumstances.

Win-win

Under this situation the following hold true.

i.   The issue is important to you;
ii.   You value the relationship with the other party;

iii.   You have enough time to search for an approach that satisfies everyone.

Win-lose

i.   The issue is important to you;
ii.   Preserving the relationship with the other party doesn't matter;
iii.   You have time to defeat the other party hands down;
iv.   You can't use a win-win solution because the other party will take advantage of you.

Lose-win

i.   The issue isn't important to you;
ii.   You value the relationship with the other party;
iii.   You are under time pressure and want to finish quickly.

Lose-lose

i.   The issue is relatively unimportant to both parties;
ii.   They may opt to build a relationship based on mutual suffering;
iii.   Time and transaction costs are usually considered as cardinal here.

Key Elements of a Good Negotiation

The Key Elements of any Negotiations are:

i.   Power

Power in a negotiation suggests that one party has what the other seeks and needs. In other words, power is the object being negotiated. It could be a raise in salary, or what is being sold at supermarket or shop etc. Power is present when something is being sought which fortunately or otherwise belongs to another.

ii.   Information

Information suggests that one of the parties knows what is at stake and is doing everything to hide the facts from the other person who is most likely unaware that the seemingly aloof and indifferent salesman for example, is concerned about making that sale as the ability to make the sale is cardinal to his progress in the organization. Background information is necessary to have an edge in the negotiation process. Each side of the negotiation should find out as much as possible what the other party stands to gain if it wins the negotiation and also what they stand to lose if they do not win the negotiation. This insight will go a long way to determining the final outcome of the negotiation process.

c.   Time

For any negotiation to be of value it must have a time limit within which to seal the deal. Some negotiators may be aware that the other party does not have time on its side and so may be more anxious to get the negotiation over and done with. The party that is aware of this will continually cause delays and appear not to be interested in the whole process thereby putting the other party on the hot spot which then makes them want to concede a lot of grounds in the negotiation to their own disadvantage. The earlier each of the parties realizes this, the better for them in resolving the issues at stake instead of playing the 'waiting game' indefinitely.

Proven Techniques for Negotiating and Resolving Conflicts

i)   Become an Observer

When you become an observer, you have the advantage of getting a better perspective of the issues at stake because you are able to listen more rather than talking. Hence, from the standpoint of being a listener you are able to observe the proceedings of a negotiation.

ii)   The Doppel-Ganger

The counsel is to empathize with the opponent's position by attempting to view issues from his perspective as well as from your own. The goal here is not to attempt to give way to him but to understand the argument from his own perspective.

iii) The Common Thread

What is entailed here is to try to find common point of agreement with the adversary and capitalize on it thereby making the opponent feel that both parties can get along after-all; this then minimizes the points of disagreement.

iv.) Low Hanging Fruit

The goal here is to concentrate on resolving the easy problems first and then to tackle the tougher problems later.

v)   The Psychologist

Here, the underlying cause of a problem is searched out and resolved instead of going around it or 'beating about the bush'. As a result, people may keep malice over certain unresolved issues, if the cause of the problem becomes apparent then to eliminate it altogether the psychologist goes direct to the root cause and attempts to solve the problem from that level. Typical situations like this arise in husband-wife relationships where for a time the cause of anger by either the husband or wife may not be known on time until much care is taken by either of the spouses to understand the situation and finding out the cause of the disagreement in order to resolve the issues ct stake.

vi.)   The Robot

Here, someone in a negotiation is cdvised to turn off his emotions and consequently refuse to cive way to it. By so doing he will be able to employ logic to look objectively at the problem at hand and to find the appropriate solution to it.

vii.   The Overflowing Cup

The overflowing cup is an encouragement to look at the good part of the other person or group and attempt to see issues more lightly on the basis of the cordial relationship that has hitherto existed between the parties and then letting this knowledge override any ill feeling for the other party. This enables concentration on positive aspects of the relationship and the ability to see issues from that perspective.

viii. Whipsaw Auction

Where there are several competitors, you should let them know that you are negotiating with them at the same time.

ix.   Big pot

Make big demands at the beginning. This ensures that you have more room for renegotiating the contract or agreement by making concessions better than if you had started from a low price.

x.   Divide and conquer

Identify a member of the negotiating team and sell him on your ideas by trying to win him to your way of thinking thereby getting him to convince other members to be on your side.

xi.   Patience

Patience is a key ingredient in any negotiation. As the saying goes, "the patient dog eats the fattest bone" The other party may require something that you only have, it is only by allowing time and patience can you achieve what you desire.

xii.   Trial Balloon

Let a third party in on your proposal to test their reactions before a final decision is made on the contract.

Parties to a Negotiation

a)   The highest- value players should be included to ensure that the deal can create the greatest possible value.

b)   The full set of potential and influential players including those that may be part of the "informal negotiations" should be reflected in the composition of the all-party-map.

c)   Those in the internal decision making and governance processes should be included to help identify potential blockers and allies.

d)   Agents who may have the wrong incentives and the ability to complicate issues should be identified in the all-party map.

Conducting a Telephone Negotiation

In conducting a telephone negotiation, a consultant should be prepared with materials at all times otherwise whatever he agrees on the telephone may become a nightmare as he may be negotiating for far less than he would have if he had been better prepared.

Whenever he submits a proposal. he should be sure to expect a telephone call anytime in respect of the contract.

However, before committing himself to anything, he should ensure that he is clear headed by telling them that he will call back to buy time for clear thinking.

When a Negotiation is Considered Successful

A negotiation is considered successful if it achieves the purposes and objectives of all the parties involved. In other words both parties must feel a sense of having achieved something worthwhile from the negotiations.

i.   The decisions reached must be the best available option. In order to have a feeling of having achieved a good deal, you need to weigh the other options on a scale to enable you consider or reflect on whether to take the options or settle for the outcome of the matter presently under negotiation. Hence your plan B should be as good as the one under negotiation in the event you have to choose this option in place of the negotiated deal.

ii.   All parties must be contented or satisfied with the out-
       come of the negotiations. For a negotiation to be con-
       sidered successful each party must go home with the
       feeling of having achieved a good deal especially if
       they can see through the benefits they could achieve
       by collaborating with one another. In this regard, each
       of the parties should look into the other's area of inter-
       est and see how it can better further mutual interest.
iii.   Have other options to select from by having more than
       one solution to the problem under negotiation, to be
       able to have more options to choose from. This enables
       you select the best possible solution.

Negotiating for a Better Deal

Negotiating for a better deal is important because the
price tag on an item may not be the real worth or value of
that item on the shelf of a supermarket or store, you could
be shortchanging yourself in the sense that although there
is a stated price and the salesman behaves as if he couldn't
care less if you purchase the item or not or that there is no
way the price could be reduced to a level affordable and
reasonable from the buyers perspective. If the attitude of
the sales personnel and price tags are taken as given, that
is, as final on the issue, you may have lost an opportunity
to have a better deal. You should always remember that
what you see on face of anything in need of a negotiation
is not the final word on it be it about issues on wages where
management says an increase is not possible, or some other matter, without going into negotiations you may never
know what could come out of it, there may be room for
an increase in workers' wages and salaries after all. Consequently, the following basic rules should be observed in
dealing with issues of negotiations or dispute resolutions.
i.   Never accept a proposal before studying the contents
       especially if the offers are too enticing and tempting.

ii.   Be bold enough to say no when you feel what is being offered does not meet expectations.

iii.   Never be intimidated by very official looking documents with iron clad statements that appear to suggest that negotiations are not welcome, you should negotiate nevertheless because in the final analysis everything is negotiable.

iv.   Let others do the negotiations. A hypertensive or emotional person may find it difficult tc keep his temper under control.

v.   In negotiating the advice is not to be guided by the body language or attitude of the other party as he may be displaying a disinterest in the whole issue being deliberated upon. One should not be fooled into thinking that he is not interested it could be a ploy!

vi.   Know where to carry on a discussion on the object of negotiation as someone may inform the other party about how enthusiastic you are to seal the deal, which could make the other party re-consider his propositions by seeking a renegotiation based on new facts now at his disposal.

v.   Deal only with someone that can make the decision and not the sales man who still reeds to consult his superiors thereby re-negoiating the entire deal all over again.

vi.   Do not feel pressured into filling up the space left by silence when the other party is considering the offer or proposal. Do not feel the need to say something because you may be losing the negotiation if you do.

Knowing the rules of a negotiation enables an understanding on how the game is played. Negotiations are better done under an atmosphere that has followed a natural and logical sequence of events leadirg to eventual round table talks where necessary. Following are probable sequences of events:

i)   Meet at a neutral setting where the other party cannot control the situation.

ii)   Find out what the other party's interest is and what he wants to achieve from the negotiation. He may demand for a certain percentage or no deal. You should not be put off to conclude that the matter cannot be approached for a re-consideration.

iii)   Develop proposals that meet the other party's' interest only after having understood the interest against your own. The purpose of this proposal should be to establish an agreement on the key issues of the negotiations.

iv)   Go forward with the bargaining process bearing in mind that you may have to concede some grounds to the other party while at the same time attempting to ensure that an organization's interest is not jeopardized by putting in place a winning agreement where all parties in the agreement will feel a sense of having achieved their objective in the whole process of negotiations.

v)   At the end of a negotiation, a definite action plan should be drawn up whereby the responsibilities and obligations of each party is clearly understood and agreed upon.

Winning a Negotiation

Negotiations cost time, efforts and resources. Someone undertaking a negotiation should be aware that although wining may be desired, sometimes however, it may be profitable to lose to enable him utilize the time, efforts and resources in propagating some other ventures that are more beneficial to him.

The issue then in a negotiation is not all about winning but about coming across to the other party and getting them to understand that although you wou d love to win, but that it would be preferable that everyone is also a winner. This in essence means that you should be willing to look at issues from your perspective as well as their own and then making concessions based on rationality of arguments and objectivity of thoughts by all parties involved in the negotiations.

Thus, in so doing, you should be willing to lose some and also win some depending on the significance of the objective desired by the other parties. Sometimes, you should also deliberately choose to lose because of stress and the kind of people you may have ˉo work with regardless of the financial rewards that may be the opportunity cost or alternative you would have to forego, thereby doing a trade off of the benefits derivable for peace of mind. Examples could be in regards to dealiˉng with stubborn or difficult customer's or clients.

Emotion and its Impact on Negotiations

Emotions are expressions of our inner feelings that become evident when we are faced with situations requiring us to make critical decisions. Emotions can be classified into positive or negative, as seen from our expressions of happiness, anger, fear etc. Negative emotions have a capacity to escalate a conflict situation as they are similar to adding fuel to an already burning fire, thereby worsening an already bad situation in need of resolution. On the other hand positive emotions help to facilitate resolution of conflicts that in turn help the attainment of individual and collective goals and objectives.

i.   Positive Emotions

As stated above, a solution is easily achievable when all parties come to the negotiating table with a positive outlook or perspective as research has shown that a positive attitude inspires the mind mechanisms to function at a more optimal level than when a negative attitude is taken to the negotiating table. Hence, people with a positive attitude exude confidence and higher tendencies in their approach to evolving a co-operative strategy that ultimately lead to the best outcomes for parties in the negotiation. When the negotiation is finally underway, those with a positive disposition are usually less contentious, and are more likely to be less aggressive in their tactics in course of seeking better gains for themselves. Negotiators with a positive mindset have been found to reach an agreement quicker than their negative or traditional counterparts. Positive negotiators are however not without their draw- backs as they tend to over rate their perception of self-performance especially with regards to achievable outcomes thereby leading to bias in reporting the outcome of the negotiation.

ii.   Negative Emotions

Negative emotions such as anger, fear etc can be detrimental to a negotiation process for any party. Negotiators who display angry emotions create more problems for the parties involved as they go to the negotiating table with an attitude implying fewer co-operations and more competition. Angry negotiators more often than not only achieve less than they can potentially achieve if they displayed a more temperate and controlled character when negotiating. Consequently, they pay less attention to issues that could have been beneficial to their interest because they have not come with an open mind that could lead to better outcomes for their own end of the bargain, instead they come with a pre-conceived idea of how they will achieve their objectives failing which they exhibit temper tantrums that eventually lead to decisions that could at best be termed average. Nevertheless anger can be beneficial as it can show the other party's minimum acceptance level suggesting ones commitments, sincerity and needs.

iii.   The other parties' emotions

Hitherto emotional discuss have been centered on the one party leaving without necessarily looking into the thought processes of the other party. It must not be taken as given that the other party will tow our line in arriving at a negotiated settlement that is acceptable to all parties involved as they also have targets to achieve. Factors that will affect a quick resolution of the issues at stake will depend on the level of trust, where there is no trust; one party will look at the other with suspicion which affects the negotiations negatively.

On the other hand when there is trust as a result of past interactions or the acceptability of the parties involved through perception and track records of honesty and sincerity in their dealings with others, it eads to an easy and quick resolution of the conflict.

Further, the need to show restraint is made more important when viewed from the backdrop of the fact that more is achieved when the effects of emotions are considered since the other party is more likely to react negatively to negative attitudes and approaches when they feel boxed into a corner with negative emotions such as anger and fear. Negative attitudes have the following effect on any negotiation.

a.   Pride; leads the other party to put up a more integrative and compromise strategy in olace.
b.   Guilt or regret; leads to better impression by the opponents as it touches on their positive emotions. However guilt or regrets could lead to a higher demand being made by the opponent.
c.   Worry and disappointments; lecd to relatively lower expectations or demand by the opponent and as a result leaves a bad impression.
d.   Anger; produces both dominating and yielding behaviors from the opponents. It however causes the opponent to place lower demands and ¬o concede more in a negotiation.

Chapter 8
The Place of Ethics in Consulting and Professional Practices

Ethics are well based standards of what is right and what is wrong. These standards are usually very specific as they prescribe the obligations, benefits to society, fairness or specific virtues of humans. Consequently, ethics may also refer to standards that compel or impose a reasonable limitation to prevent the commission of societal vices such as rape, murder, stealing, fraud, assault, slander & fraud as well as encouraging virtues such as honesty, loyalty compassion etc. In addition, ethics includes the constant measuring of ethical issues against norms and practices. This entails looking introspectively at one's own behaviour pattern with a view to correcting or aligning it in such a way that there is a clear definition of what is clearly right or wrong.

Importance of Ethics to Consulting Practices

Ethics is important to consulting practices because without it, what is expected from an individual or organization may be difficult to determine. Organizational or professional ethics sets out the mode of comportment expected of the members of a given profession, say, law, medicine, accounting, diplomacy etc. that is, organizational ethics spells out clearly what is expected from practitioners of a given profession as well as sanctions for behaviours that fall short of the acceptable standards set out by the profession concerned. For instance ethical situations arise:

a)   Where a client seeks confirmation of what he or she already knows;

b)   Where a client wants the consultant to doctor, edit or omit the findings to suit what he or she wants;

c)   Where the client seeks information from his consultant about competitors;

d)   Where the intention of the engagement is to present a false report to the management of a company or organization when a staff at a lower level seeks help in trying to deceive either the superiors, management and board of directors;

e)   Where a recruiting agency's assent is being sought in order to recommend the employment of a lesser quali-fied candidate at the expense of a more qualified or competent candidate.

f)   Where a consultant is requested to falsify a document to suit the client.

Misconceptions about Ethics

There are several misconceptions about what ethics is or what is entailed in the practice of ethics. Some of these misconceptions are explained below.

i.   Religion
A religion is a pattern or system of belief that is held by a group of people and it governs and affects their way of life as addressed by the tenets of that religion. Religious bodies

operate within the ambit of state laws and are of several types, some of which include Christianity, Islam, Hinduism, Buddhism as well as Atheism. These al have different and similar patterns of worship and belief and their followers are taught the tenets of the religion in order to guide their lives towards the end result of the life hereafter. The codes of conduct such as living in peace with the neighbours, love and kindness, courage set by these religions are part of ethics but do not necessarily encapsulate all that is entailed by ethics as it involves much more.

ii.   Law

All spheres of the human endeavour are governed by law especially as instituted by the government. Law is useful for the control and regulation of a society in order to keep its citizens in check to enable them promote and propagate the norms of a society regarding what is right and what is wrong. As a result laws set out ethical standards of comportment and behaviours expected of the citizenry. But while ethics is a part and parcel of the laws of a society, it cannot cover the whole gamut of ethics. For instance slavery, may serve the interest of nations and individuals who are beneficiaries, but is it ethical to enslave another fellow human? The obvious answer is no; the apartheid era and the issues of seizure of the land of white minority farmers in Zimbabwe are good examples.

iii.   Societal expectations

Ethics is not the same thing as doing what society expects of us. People can be affected by peer pressure and as such expectations from society influences the way they behave. Consequently, what is right or wrong is determined through the prism with which the society looks at issues. Again, what is right in one society may be considered wrong in another. Take the issue of marriage for instance where one is entitled to one wife and another society where it is legal to marry more than one. All have acted within the bounds of what society accepts and therefore looking at ethical issues from these perspectives will not encapsulate all there is to say about ethics.

iv.   Feelings
There are also misconceptions that ethics is synonymous with feelings. What a person feels is right may actually turn out to be the wrong action when executed. Hence, feelings or hunches may not capture the real meaning of ethics as it is again much more than these. Feelings are not static they do change depending on the circumstances one is being faced with. It is this shifting nature of feelings and its bi-products that make it unrealistic to refer to ethics as feelings.

Codes of Ethics in Research

Following are some codes of ethics that govern research and certain aspects of interactions with other fellow humans.

i.   Honesty,
ii.   Objectivity,
iii.   Integrity,
iv.   Carefulness,
v.   Openness,
vi.   Respect for intellectual property,
vii.   Confidentiality,
viii. Responsible publication,
ix.   Responsible mentoring,
x.   Respect for colleagues,
xi.   Social Responsibility,
xii.   Non discrimination,
xiii. Competence,
xiv.   Legality,

xv.   Animal care,
xvi. Human subject protection.

The Purpose of Ethics

As a result of the criminal convictions of insider traders in the 1980's which resulted in the collapses of Enron, World-Com, and Arthur Andersen, the mutual funds trading scandals, the revelations of the accounting fraud ,and Martha Stewart have made a study of ethics in organizations and schools the world over imperative.

The purpose of ethics in an organization is to make practitioners aware of the ethical implications of organizational decisions. This may be achieved in schools through case studies and role playing by students as they confront ethical dilemmas similar to those they will face in a real world situation.

Topics that may generate interesting discussions include:

i.   Corporate restructuring and the consequences of lay-offs.
ii.   Issues on diversity such as race, gender, ethnicity, and sexual orientation.
iii. Issues that bother on employee privacy, e.g. Sexual harassment, HIV and AIDS, Drug testing etc.
iv.   Issues on the environment such as green house emissions, and pollutions, dumping of toxic waste materials and animal rights etc.
v.   MNC's and their conduct on issues such as bribery of government officials to obtain contract awards.

vi.   Other issues such as anti-thrust actions, insider trading, predatory pricing etc.

Relativism Vs Stakeholder's theory

Relativism

Relativism attempts to explain why ethical issues come up and why ethics is usually avoided in reaching decisions. Stakeholder's analysis on the other hand seeks to provide a structure for confronting ethical decisions that are made on behalf of an organization. There are basically 7 classifications of relativism namely:

i.   Role relativism,
ii.   Naïve relativism,
iii.   Cultural relativism,
iv.   Social group relativism,
v.   Natural laws,
vi.   Utilitarianism,
vii.   Universalism.
       Role Relativism

Role relativism refers to the difference between someone's private self and the roles he may exhibit publicly. That is, it is quite possible to live a dual lifestyle, often the direct opposite of the other. That is, the role he plays may prevent him from taking steps to correct what he knows to be ethically wrong. For instance, members of the top management of an organization may be in support of the actions of its employees in organizing a strike action but they may not be seen to be on the side of the employees by giving this support openly but must at all times argue in favor of the organization as a result of the position or "role" they may play even against their better judgment and beliefs.

Naïve Relativism

Naïve relativism holds out that an individual makes decisions based on what he thinks is right or wrong, which has been processed through his own decision making mechanism and thought processes. Hence, his decisions should not be a subject of debate or discussion as to whether he made the right decision or not because he alone knows what went into making the decision that he has executed. In other words, no one is qualified to suggest that a better decision could have been made given the circumstances faced by someone no matter his credentials or experience. Organization A's management may therefore not be qualified to judge the actions of organization B's management on issues that are common to both companies as what their experiences and challenges are may be completely different.

Cultural Relativism

Cultural relativism indicates that what is right in Country A may be considered wrong in country B. Multinational companies may have to adopt the adage" when in Rome do as the Romans....." approach to be able to fit into a society and to even make a headway. This may then lead them into giving bribes to obtain contracts as the effect of bribes is to sway support in favour of an organization. Further, the way of life such as language, food, dressings etc are sacred to a people; it will therefore be unthinkable to regard their practices as inferior to one's own simply because they are dissimilar. However, some countries such as the US and Germany have instituted legislations that make it criminal to adopt practices in host countries by MNC's that are not in conformity with the practices of the country of origin of the companies seeking business opportunities in another.

Social Group Relativism

This is similar to Naïve relativism in the sense that people are likely to rationalize their actions or inactions by making references to societal norms like "club rule", "professional codes of conduct", "industry best practices", "accepted practices", etc.

Utilitarianism

This suggests that the rightness or wrongness of a certain action or inaction of a person or group of people is dependent on the utility or reward to be gained from such an action or inaction. That is "the end justifies the means" or "the greatest good for the greatest number"

Natural laws

Natural laws refer to actions that are justified by the belief that they are either right or wrong and adjudged to be so based principally on what nature or the Bible or some other Holy books have to say about such an action or inaction.

Universalism

Universalism is a system of belief that all people can and will be saved. Many religions hold this view and belief that there is a day of reckoning when everyone will be asked to account for how he has lived his life on earth whether doing right or doing wrong by the standards of the religion. Universalism therefore holds the belief that all actions are condonable if the motive behind the action is good.

Stakeholder's Theory

Stakeholders' theory is an attempt to ensure the corporate survival of an organization especially with regards to its reason for being in existence. This theory holds that for any organization, there are several people who have a stake in ensuring its survival and these people must be considered in making or carrying out any decisions. Failure to do this may have a disastrous effect on the growth and stability of the firm.

The following are some stakeholders an organization will do well to pay attention to their needs and wants to enable it integrate all that have a stake in the organization. These are:

a)   Employees-are interested in their salaries and welfare packages as well as a career prospect with the organization in such a way as to ensure that they can continue working with the organization for as long as they wish to.

b)   Shareholders—are interested in the size and quality of the dividend that will likely accrue to them as owners of a company.

c)   Bondholders- are interested in the ability of the organization to honour the terms of agreement of the bond or mortgage taken by the organization to finance its investment activities.

d)   Creditors-want to be sure that there is enough cash flow in the organization to pay for goods and services supplied to the organization in order to ensure timely payment in their favour.

e)   Government-is interested in job creation as well as tax-
      es on the profits of the organization to enable it gener-
      ate more income for the state.

f)   Environmentalists- are interested in the protection of
      the environment from the consequences of the ac-
      tions of companiess as they seek out raw materials for
      the manufacture and production of goods and ser-
      vices which may have a negative impact on the envi-
      ronment, such as the pollution of air and water, green
      house emissions and the attendant effects on climate
      change etc.

g)   The immediate community- is interested in what is in
      the whole deal for them. The companies therefore
      have a responsibility to ensure that the community
      from which they generate their income is well taken
      care of by ploughing back some of its profits into meet-
      ing some of its socio economic needs thereby assisting
      government in providing succour for the people as a
      responsible corporate citizen.

h)   Competitors- These want to see the performance of ri-
      vals and would also relish negative consequences of
      actions of such organizations to enable them obliter-
      ate any competition.

i)   Clients- are interested in the benefits they will derive
      from the use of the organization's service and also the
      price at which they are able to get these services com-
      pared to that of the competition.

j)   Executive board of directors-are interested in perpetu-
      ating their existence in office and will resist all actions
      that may necessitate their removal from office in the
      event of non-performance. They are also interested in

continuing in office because of the perks of office that are due to them.

Catering for all Interest Groups

Actions by companies seeking to ensure that all interest groups are adequately catered for will include:

i.   Identifying the main cast of participants or characters.
ii.   Identifying the benefits as well as the harm that may affect each party.
iii. Determining the rights and obligations of the parties.
iv.   Weighing the powers held by each of the parties.
v.   Analyzing the short and long term effects of decisions being made.
vi.   Setting and seeking alternative plans in the event there is a need to modify the first plan.
vii. Deciding on the appropriate course of action to take and implement.

The United States legislature in order to ensure that ethics is at the fore front of operations of companies enacted an act designed to regulate how these organizations are operated. Accordingly, Sarbanes Oxley's act of 2002 came into effect as a result of the corporate scandals that rocked American companies such as Arthur Andersen, ImClone, Enron, Adelphi, and Credit Suisse, WorldCom etc. in and around the world. Other Countries such as Nigeria put in place the Nigerian Deposit Insurance Corporation (NDIC) which has the responsibility for seeing to it that banks have enough deposits to ensure that depositors do not lose their moneys or investments in the event of liquidation and bankruptcy. Other measures that have been taken in recent times include the consolidation and recapitalization of banks in Nigeria with a minimum capital base of N25 Billion Naira, to help shore up the ability of these banks to compete in the global arena.

There are basically four areas that are addressed by Sarbanes Oxley's act:

1. Financial accounting rules
i.   Audit committees consist of independent directors and at least one financial expert.
ii. The chief executive officers and chief financial officers are required to co-sign and certify that the financial statement present a true and fair view of the financial activities of the organization.
iii. The powers to establish new public accounting over-sight board should reside with the Securities and Ex-change Commission.

2. Internal control Rules
i.   The workings of the system of internal control in respect of financial reporting should be certified by CEO's and CFO's.
ii. The strength and weaknesses of the system of internal control operating in an organization must be certified by independent external auditors.
3. Executive Ethical Conduct Rules
i.   Senior executives are required to adopt a code of ethi-cal conduct for themselves.
ii. Loans must not be granted by public companies to ex-ecutive officers or directors.
iii. When financial statements do not conform to expected standards, when re-done, culpable CEO's and CFO's may be required to return compensation's received by them.
iv. Stocks should not be traded during pension fund black-outs periods by directors, and other insider's.

v.   Whistle blowing protection for corporate executives who report misdeeds of companies and their management.
4.   Ethical conduct rules for related parties.
i.   New professional responsibilities for lawyers.
ii.   New conflict of interest rules for financial analysts.

Corporate Governance

Because of the apparent importance of the economic health of corporations and societies as a whole, corporate governance has become imperative and a subject of interest to all and sundry. Corporate governance can be defined as the process of instituting a responsible form of management in an organization whereby it is run in a fashion that is transparent and accountable. In this manner, a structure is put in place which specifies the distribution of rights and responsibilities among different participants such as the board, managers, shareholders and other stakeholders spelling out the manner and ways for reaching decisions on corporate affairs. The whole essence of the above is to provide a structure for setting objectives and reaching organizational goals.

Many Capital markets across the world have instituted one form of corporate governance or the other to enable them direct and control the affairs and activities of the markets. For example the UK and US Capital markets have a varied ownership structure when compared to the centralized systems found in many countries the world over. Consequently, the pattern of ownership greatly determines the way in which policy maker's deal with issues of corporate governance and the management of potential conflicts of interest between ownership and control of the organization, often referred to as the 'Principal/Agency' problem.

In a widely dispersed ownership structure such as in the US and UK, conflicts occur as a result of the tendency for control between the Principals-Owners of companies, and Agents—Board of directors, these all have their areas of interest and focus which may affect the decisions that they may make on behalf of their company. A centralized ownership's conflicts arise from the owner's and majority shareholders seeking to promote their own interests above that of the minority shareholders through the use of voting powers on issues that ultimately will be in favour of the majority shareholders.

In this respect, corporate governance is designed to act as a means of succour for shareholders through:

i.   The protection of their rights;
ii.   Enhancement of disclosure and transparency;
iii. Facilitation of the effective functioning of the board of directors;
iv.   Provision of efficient legal and regulatory enforcement framework.

Thus, the Principal/Agency is addressed through a combination of law, stock exchange listing rules and self regulatory codes.

Further, different approaches to corporate governance issues have been adopted by many countries, since 'stakeholders' have a critical role to play as they are given the benefits of making their inputs at a stakeholders meeting which has become the trend these days, thereby promoting collective governance. The US and the UK however, have in times past tended to continue the traditional approach of creating wealth principally for the shareholders which is their area of focus. However, all countries abreast with corporate governance issues have shown an appreciation for OECD's (Organization for Economic Co-operation and Development) work in the area of transparency, responsibility, accountability, and fairness.

- Transparency

Transparency requires an organization to be directed in such a way that its activities are not shrouded in secrecy as to make others feel that something ulterior may be going on. Hence, the organization's directors must make conscious efforts to ensure that al who need information on the operational and financial processes of the organization are not denied access.

- Responsibility

Suggest that the actions of the board of directors of the organization should be carefully weighed against various interest groups in the organization before they are taken. In this way, only decisions that have passed through proper analysis and contemplation will likely be implemented.

- Accountability

The board of directors and management of the organization must at all times see itself as a steward of the resources put under them by constantly being reminded that they are only custodians of the investments of others counting on it to grow the organization on their behalf.

- Fairness

Actions taken and board of directors must be seen to be fair to all the stakeholders of the organization; as such they must weigh the interest of the various parties be they, clients, employees, shareholders, directors themselves, government, the immediate community, etc.

Why Corporate Governance is Important

Corporate governance is significant for the following reasons:

i.   It helps to enhance an investor's confidence in an organization as he feels that the organization is not being run or managed in an arbitrary fashion. In this way, competition is encouraged thereby improving economic growth and wellbeing of the organization.

ii.   The forces behind Globalization have more than ever made it imperative for a better structure for managing companies to be put in place. As a result, corporate governance can help in the area of improved technology, and private sector development through increasing capital flows to developing economies which in turn leads to a wider market opportunity that will eventually need stabilizing legislation such as corporate governance to ensure investor confidence which is necessary for the injection of more capital by these investors as a result of the global confidence in the markets.

iii. Corporate Scandals—have led to the erosion of the confidence of investors as a result of misreporting of financial facts by companies such as ENRON and Arthur Andersen and others, thereby having a negative impact on investments by the public.

iv.   Shareholder activism—these arise when institutions invest in companies, consequently if an organization goes under, the institutions themselves may likely go bankrupt. In order to ensure that their investments are well managed, they take active interest in how the companies, in which they have re-invested client's funds, are properly managed.

Chapter 9
How to manage and Influence people

People are cardinal to any worthwhile achievement or any endeavour because they are the fulcrum upon which an organization revolves. To achieve desired objectives every organization is duty bound to ensure that they are armed with the proper tools to be able to give back to the system or organization. Thus, people management is central to the activities of organizations depending on the size and number of employees of a firm which involves helping them reach their potential through carefully laid out instructional patterns of managing and delegation of tasks and duties.

Management is an art as well as a science. It is an art in that it helps people to be more efficient in the performance of any task through effective supervision and adequate motivation to perform the tasks as desired. It is also a science because management has its own methodology on how it can achieve its goals and objectives. As a result, management functions such as planning, directing, organizing, and control, staffing, budgeting, coordinating and reporting are often referred to as the 'Pillars of Management'.

Functions of Management

Managers principally perform the following 5 basic functions which are discussed below.

1.   Planning

Planning is the act of formulating a program for a definite course of action. Proper planning entails creative thinking and the production of a blueprint on which management decisions are going to be based. Effective planning entails setting out clearly the vision, mission, goals, objectives, strategy of an organization.

To plan therefore is to be forward looking as it is often said that "he who fails to plan, plans to fail". Proper planning is required for any worthwhile venture as it is the precursor to setting the tone for the project at hand. Thus, a plan is like a map that guides an individual, company or organization in determining where it is, where it wants to be and how it can get to its desired destination or target in the most cost efficient means possible. When the organization knows where it is, it becomes easier to make decisions on where it wants to go and what it wants to do next. We shall discuss more about planning under strategy in chapter 12.

2.   Directing

No one likes to get lost. Likewise, directing as a function of management requires that the ship of an organization be run in such a way as to engender focus and cohesiveness in achieving set aims and objectives of the organization. To direct effectively, management needs to put in place a system that motivates, communicate, promotes and encourages group dynamics, and which raises and trains leaders through discipleship and discipline. Directing involves influencing people's behaviour. Several terminologies have been used to describe this management function, some of which include leadership, motivat on, interpersonal relations, and influencing people among others.

- Leadership

Leadership requires self confidence in order to make decisions, motivate others and take responsibility for one's actions no matter the outcome. To be an effective leader, one needs to overcome the fears, as well as anxieties over losing control of a business or orgcnization. In addition, many of the fears exhibited by those in a position of leadership stem from the fear of insanity, fear of failure and of embarrassing themselves before others.

Fears can either be positive or negative. Positive fears derive from the consequences of actions we know are punishable by the authorities or those in control over us. Such fears could be as a result of the commission of murder, fraud, or other social vices etc. Negative fears on the other hand are really another form of worry. So long as one fails to gain control over worry, negative fear will constantly lurk around like a plague waiting to pounce upon a prey. In order words, to be an effective leader, one must forget oneself by dealing with the perceived weaknesses and also acknowledging that everyone has fears but the difference is in the way each person handles and deals with his fears.

Ralph Waldo Emerson aptly puts this in its proper perspective "Do the things you fear and the death of fear is certain". And that "fears spring from ignorance" That is, the cure for fear is, to act contrary to our (negative) fears, as the things we fear more often than not do not occur. Of course, the things we fear may be a result of the type of childhood we may have had, nevertheless, anyone desirous of overcoming his fears, can do so if he is serious and committed to taking appropriate steps to solving his problems by looking within himself and analysing the reasons why he is that way to enable him make use of the prescribed cures that have been successful with others. "Fear is never a reason for quitting, it's only an excuse..." Says Norman Vincent Peale, the Author of the Power of Positive Thinking.

Further, many literatures have been written on self improvement and anyone having spasms of fear would do well to avail himself of any of these books. "Who moved my cheese" authored by Johnson is an excellent read for anyone seeking to understand the reason for change as well as the process of change. He counsels with the use of examples from mice and little people caught in a maze that in the face of a changing world, one should take steps that are affirmative by proactively accepting change as part of life and dealing with it accordingly, as accepting and managing change prepares one to be more productive and free from the paralyzing effects of fear and anxiety.

In addition, the habit of keeping oneself organized by keeping a daily -to -do lists helps check those things that have been successfully accomplished during the course of the day thereby giving a feeling of being productive. An up-to-date contact list also helps in networking and keeping connected with friends and associates. Stephen R. Covey, in the book "Seven habits of highly effective people" recommends that people should take responsibility, make up their minds about what is pertinent and stick to it. Other Life (Leadership) coaches suggest the creation of a detailed set of goals for oneself, organization, professional relationships, family relationships, and the community. Yet others suggest that someone grappling with leadership problems should take the following prescribed steps:

a) Find his own voice and calling as well as inspiring other people to find their voices.
b) Do regular exercises; keep healthy eating and social habits.
c) Smile more as the one who smiles makes other people happy and by implication receives back happiness.

d)   Cut back on caffeine, smoking and ensure a proper
     sleeping habit.

• Motivation

Motivation explains the reason for the way we behave
or act. It gives an insight into how employees react to stimu-
lus in response to incentives from their employers whether
in cash or in kind. Abraham Irvin Maslow in his Hierarchical
theory of needs opines that human needs are hierarchical,
that is, they are progressive in the sense that as one level of
needs are met and satisfied he seeks to also satisfy the next
level of needs. He arranged these needs in the famous Hierarchical triangle of needs. In this triangle Maslow proposes
five levels of needs which are interconnected.

a.   Physiological needs; include the need for food, cloth-
     ing, shelter, sex, sleep, and excretion etc.
b.   Safety; the security of life and property, of employment,
     of family etc.
c.   Love/belonging; the need for friendship, love and inti-
     macy.
d.   Self esteem; people want to be respected and as such
     appreciated. They crave for self esteem, and self con-
     fidence.
e.   Self actualization; at this level of need someone expe-
     riences satisfaction, and is generally contented with
     what he has been able to achieve and is generally
     creative, spontaneous, more able to accept facts as
     presented to him based on objectivity and is also not
     biased.

Maslow classified the first four levels of needs as deficiency needs. These needs according to him must be met so
as not to make someone anxious. In themselves, the needs
do not appear to add anything to the state of well-being
of someone but are pertinent to ensuring that he at least
meets the basic needs. The last or fifth level of needs is re-

garded as growth needs which presuppose that someone having already satisfied the 'D' needs will naturally want to grow and consolidate. Growth needs or 'B' needs are not only for humans but also for companies which apart from the basic goal of maximizing profits or shareholders value also seek growth.

- Victor Vroom's Expectancy Theory

Expectancy theory teaches that a person's motivation is based on three factors, namely:

i.   Valence,

Valence signifies how important the outcome of an effort is to a person such that he is motivated to for instance, do the cleaning for a friend. The outcome is usually seen as a reward which may be tangible, like money, or intangible, like knowing that one has done a good job.

ii.   Expectancy

Expectancy implies that the effort put into something is related to the end. Assuming that the reward for doing the cleaning is the promise of lunch in a prominent restaurant, One's motivation would depend on how desirable having such a lunch is. The need for the lunch will determine the level of motivation to complete the task.

iii.   Instrumentality

To be motivated to do the cleaning, one would have to believe that efforts put in will lead to the envisaged results. Consequently, the tools for doing the cleaning must be present, such as detergent, water and or electricity to power the vacuum cleaner or washing machine as the case may be. Instrumentality therefore leads to the realization that the end product will affect the rewards that a person receives.

Thus, to be motivated, one would have to believe that by doing the cleaning one would get the promised reward. The expectancy theory suggests that the presence of all three factors go a long way to determine if one will be motivated to complete a task. Consequently, the absence of one or more of these factors may hinder the completion of the task.

- Frederick Herzberg's Two Factor Hygiene Theory

In the book "The motivation to work" Herzberg shows the relationship between employee attitude and motivation which result in either satisfaction or dissatisfaction. He conducted a study that indicated that the factors causing satisfaction were different from those causing dissatisfaction. Consequently, he developed the motivation- hygiene theory to explain the results of the findings. He gave the appellation "motivators" to those factors that lead to employee satisfaction (satisfiers) and "hygiene" to those that lead to dissatisfaction (dissatisfiers). The term hygiene is used to express a means whereby employee dissatisfaction is ameliorated through maintenance since their grievances cannot altogether be eradicated or addressed wholly.

Following are factors in their order of importance that cause employee dissatisfaction and satisfaction.

Dissatisfiers	Satisfiers
i. Company policy	i. Achievement
ii. Supervision	ii. Recognition
iii. Relationship with Boss	iii. Work itself
iv. Work conditions	iv. Recognition

| v. Salary | v. Advancement |
| vi. Relationship with peers | vi. Growth |

Further, Herzberg argues that human needs are significant in determining physiological needs which may be satisfied with for instance money to purchase food; clothing, rent a house etc. on one hand and physiological needs which can only be satisfied by those things that lead to growth itself, on the other. Consequently, he asserts that the opposite of for instance, satisfaction is not necessarily dissatisfaction but non-satisfaction. In like manner the opposite of dissatisfaction is not satisfaction, but no satisfaction.

In addition, Herzberg explains that using the *Carrot and Stick* approach, that is, the process of providing incentive to cause employees to act in a certain manner, only serves as a temporary palliative to a deep sited desire or need for employees to satisfy their physiological needs. In other words, motivator factors that lead to satisfaction or dissatisfaction are part and parcel of the job themselves.

•   Lessons for Management

In view of Herzberg's theory, management is expected to provide the needed impetus in the form of hygiene factors to prevent dissatisfaction of employees and to encourage them by providing work based incentive to ensure job satisfaction. Thus, Herzberg opines that in order to achieve intrinsic motivation, organization's must first put in place a continuous program or system of job enrichment which should have:

a.   Sufficient job challenge to enable full utilization of employee skills and knowledge;

b.   A basis for matching hardworking employees who display increasing levels of ability with increasing levels of responsibilities.

c.   A basis for automating or getting a lower level employee to do any job that cannot fully utilize the skills of another employee to prevent the situation where they begin to become de-motivated.

However, Herzberg's theory has been criticized for its two pronged approach, with critics insisting that it is natural for people to desire praise or credit for satisfaction and to blame dissatisfaction on factors they consider beyond their control. In addition, they also opine that job satisfaction does not in any way imply a high level of motivation or productivity. Nevertheless, its real worth may be in the recognition of the fact that true motivation comes from within an employee and not from threat.

Why People Behave the Way they Do

When people interact they unconsciously require the other parties to be obligated to keeping their words. This expectation is cardinal to fostering and nurturing the process of exchange of material and non- material goods and services. Hence, the need for good individual and interpersonal relationship in and outside the work environment to facilitate interdependence and mutual obligation to an organization, thereby promoting its stability, growth and development cannot be over-emphasized.

Following are the reasons why people behave the way they do and are accounts for why people who sometimes behave in the same way would also act differently given certain or different circumstances. A manager therefore needs to understand these differences and their dynamics to appreciate the magnitude of his task of getting them to relate and work harmoniously with one another.

i.   Individual personality traits,

ii.   Aims and aspirations,
iii.   Interest,
iv.   Traditions,
v.   Attitudes,
vi.   Culture,
vii. Values,
viii. Preferences and biases,

In addition to the above, the under-listed factors also affect the way individuals act and behave in an organization.

i.   Organizational system of communication,
ii.   Leadership role and style,
iii.   The motivation and morale of employees,
iv.   Existing relationship between supervisors and subordinates,
v.   Existing opportunities for self development and self actualisation,
vi.   The extent of participation of employees in the affairs of the organization, in terms of its decision making and planning.

How to Manage Interpersonal Relationship

Leadership in the work environment is primarily concerned with influencing behaviour of staff. This is shown in the areas of:

i.   Supervision of subordinates,
ii.   Mode of communication in the organization,
iii.   Resolution of crisis and conflicts in the organization,
iv.   Decision making and decision taking,
v.   Guidance and counselling.

To properly manage interpersonal relationships in an organization, leaders or managers must ensure that the work environment or atmosphere is free from rancour, suspicion and lack of trust among the various levels of staff of the organization. A sound and cordial relationship is the key to achieving the best from employees. In these ways, employees can both achieve the goals of the organizations as well as their own through mutual co-operation where each one sees himself as a part of a harmonious setting where his interest is also being taken into consideration in achieving the goals of the organization. This then frees the system from negative attitudinal and behavioural factors such as:

i.   Tension and constant conflicts,
ii.   Antagonism,
iii.   Unhealthy rivalry,
iv.   Personal vendetta,
v.   Lack of meaningful communication.

In conclusion, managers and leaders have a duty to lead by example by creating c conducive work environment through service and effective leadership that promotes sound and positive interpersonal relationships between employees and themselves. This also entails managers having a good understanding of the human personality in such a way as to be able to help the subordinates and employees of the organization in reaching their objectives and full potentials.

Chapter 10
How Organisation's put their Affairs in Order

In organizing and coordinating their affairs, most firms structure their organizations along the following lines:

a.   Division of labor

Division of labor means that work is divided in such a way that no one single individual starts and completes a job alone. Division of labour is a particular form of specialization whereby tasks are assigned to individuals better competent in any field which usually become their area of competence. Adam Smith in his book "The Wealth of Nations" was of the view that cs society grows the extent to which this growth can be attained wil be dependent on the ability to specialize by the sub-division of the tasks that are capable of increasing efficiency and effectiveness of production. Frederick Tailor was also of the disposition that workers soon become experts in their jobs and by implication competent and more productive in tangible outputs produced by them.

b.   Departmentation

Departmentation means that an organization may be divided into separate segments or units called departments, such as administration, human resource management, finance and accounts, research & development departments, marketing etc. thereby making them better organized and reporting lines become better understood as responsibilities are assigned to schedule Officers. Other examples include, stores offering specialised services and sale of household product and appliances, often referred to as departmental stores such as Auchan, Carrefour, and Macro etc. in France and Belgium.

c.   Delegation of duties

Delegation is inevitable if things are to go well in an organization. It is a process of training subordinates by getting things done through them. In other words, it is impossible to speak of management without talking of delegation of duties. Delegation is required because everything cannot be done at the same time. Top Management needs to delegate assignments to responsible Officers to enable them (Management) concentrate on policy and decision making matters. By delegating activities, the Chief executive entrusts his authority and gives subordinates the freedom to employ their knowledge and ideas in solving or resolving issues through generating ideas and solutions to problems being faced by the organization.

d.   Span of control

Span of control is the number of subordinates under the supervision of a manager which could range between one -to -ten as the case may be. The more the people to be supervised the more the level of the responsibility to be borne by him to ensure successful outcomes for his organization. However, the optimal span of control is difficult to tell? Consequently, many assumptions and theories have been postulated which suggest that it is a function of knowledge, ability and resourcefulness of the organization and people concerned.

Staffing

Staffing entails recruitment of competent and qualified personnel to carry out various tasks required to help
an organization achieve its goals for being in existence. It
involves hiring the right calibre of personnel to man various
positions in the organization and finding, evaluating, establishing and building working relationships between future
staff and colleagues in the organization or project. It also includes the firing of such staff however unpleasant this may
be when they are no longer needed.

- Finding the right calibre of staff

Finding the right staff is not an easy task, but it is not
insurmountable. The right employee is required in every position or opening in an organization to make it go right; a
case of putting the right peg in the right holes. The right
staff can be found through recruitment of appropriate and
qualified personnel through interviews, submission of résu-
mé or curriculum vitae or through the use of head-hunters
or recruitment agencies whose specialization is finding the
right people to take up the positions in an organization.

- Qualities of a Prospective Employee

a.   Integrity

To have integrity is for one to be back of his words by
matching words with actions. Integrity cannot be divorced
from one's character as it can only be built through a consistent and positive pattern of behaviour. People with integrity take responsibility for their actions as they are quite
conversant with the laws of their organization enough to
ensure that they do not run foul of it. These kinds of people

tell the truth and are often seen as the conscience of their organizations.

b.   Intelligence

Intelligence must not be confused with education and it is that ability to make curious inquisitions into any problematic situation or difficulty and get it solved. In order words, intelligence can be hereditary or acquired through training and is not a function of the school or university one has attended.

c.   Maturity

Maturity essentially means the ability to withstand heat and to also handle stress and setbacks. Maturity is not a function of age as anyone can be mature irrespective of his or her age. A mature person shows that he can enjoy life by giving and reaching out to others and helping them reach their potentials. Immature people are often irritable and impatient. Patience comes with maturity as this singular virtue more often than not holds the key to the resolution of many a problematic situation both in the office and in our homes.
Patience must not be confused for inaction or procrastination. Procrastination is waiting and eventually doing nothing or acting at the wrong time, while patience is to know what to say and do at the right time and in the right way. To be a go -getter by thriving on action and encouraging change, one must be an optimist by being a good conversationalist and also have the capacity and ability to make friends easily by being happy and energetic always.

•   Terms of Employment in Bureaucratic Organizations

i.   Official are employed on the basis of a contract and have their personal freedom.
ii.   Officials are not elected but appointed.
iii.   Professional qualification is crucial to being employed.
iv.   Officials may be appointed on, contract, temporary as well as permanent and pensionable basis.
v.   Promotion is based on merit, seniority and examinations score as in the case of the Federal Civil Service of Nigeria. A career structure also exists.
vi.   Discipline of officials is done through a unified control and disciplinary system that defines clearly the means of compulsion and its exercise by relevant authorities such as the senior staff committee and the Federal Civil Service Commission.

• Evaluating Employees and Organizational Performances

Performance evaluation is the process of achieving a collaborative effort between employees and managers. What makes a performance evaluation successful is the actual performance conversation that a manager has with employees concerning the achievement of organizational objectives. Performance evaluation process is designed to achieve the:

a)   The alignment of employee performance with unit and organization mission anc goals;
b)   The promotion of a two-way communication regarding job performance and periodic assessment of goals and opportunities for the unit and the individual;
c)   Establishment of a mutually-understood set of performance expectations;
d)   Recognition of contributions of employees;
e)   Discussion of opportunities for growth and development, and;

f)   Provision of necessary feedback when performance does not meet expectations.

- Criteria for Measuring Public Sector performance

The following criteria are employed to measure performance in the public sector.

1)   Efficiency;
2)   Effectiveness;
3)   Economy;

The Efficiency Criteria

It is no gainsaying that the success or failure of Government activities is largely dependent on the level of efficiency of its workforce and its system of getting things done. Simply put, efficiency is the relationship that exists between output and input. In other words, efficiency is the measure of output to input and can be expressed as the ratio of output to input. If more outputs are achieved for fewer inputs, it may be safely concluded that the resources of an organization have been properly utilised. Whenever efficiency is expressed in input it is expressed as cost per unit of output. In order to improve efficiency management may decide to achieve this through the following strategies:

a)   Increasing the output of its production for an equivalent amount of input;
b)   Decreasing the amount of input for an equivalent amount of output;
c)   Increasing output by a larger proportion than proportionate increase in input;
d)   Decreasing input by a larger proportion than an equivalent proportion of increase.

The Economy Criteria

The word economy refers to ability of managers to achieve cost savings by utilizing fewer resources to achieve the required level of output. Consequently, the measure of success a manager achieves will be dependent on whether the project under consideration costs more or less than the budget and whether the project is comparatively cost effective when compared with other similar projects.

The Effectiveness Criteria

This is mainly concerned with output measurement only especially in the achievement of the objectives of the organization in physical units. Effectiveness does not mention the actual expenditure value used to achieve the result but is rather concerned with whether the initial objective sought to be achieved were eventually met as anything to the contrary renders the project ineffective.

Inter-relationship between the 3 E's

i.   Economy concerns itself with input results in a country's currency; say the U.S Dollar, Euro, or Naira. On the other hand, effectiveness involves the measurement of physical output targets while efficiency measures the relationship between both output and input.

ii.   Economy may be detrimental to the attainment of set out objectives in the sense that it may be possible to obtain an item economically, but it is another matter entirely whether the item purchased meets the standard or objective sought to be achieved.

iii. Likewise the concept of effectiveness has limitation in its use alone and depends on the achievement of sought objectives as anything to the contrary suggests financial losses of great proportion.

All of these three measures of evaluating performance are what is often referred to as 'value for money' which basically relates output to inputs.

Control

To control is to exercise authority or dominating influence over an assigned area of duty or task. There are basically four parts to control, and they include:

i)   Determining the organization's objectives,
ii)   Measuring and reporting actual performance,
iii)   Comparing the objectives and performance of the organization, and,
iv)   Taking corrective or preventive action.

The organization's objectives or performance standards are the benchmarks upon which it can plan for results. Appropriate standards should be set for important tasks and care should be taken to avoid the temptation of lowering such standards unduly, unless it is proven that the standards set compared to what obtains in the industry is unrealistic. If this is the case, corrective actions need to be taken to address any anomalies and to rectify the identified problem.

   •   Characteristics of the Control Process

Control has a circular flow to it because as performance standards are set, they are executed and monitored to observe whether there are variances, which could either be positive or negative. Controls cover all aspects of an organization and includes the control of the production, marketing, finance as well as the human resource aspects, among others.

An effective system of control involves: controls at all levels of an organization, flexibility, acceptability to those who enforce decisions, accuracy, timeliness, and understandability, balance between objectivity and subjectivity, cost effectiveness, coordination with planning, organizing and leading. It needs to be mentioned however, that care should be taken not to make controlling a bureaucratic issue to the extent that the essence of establishing a system of controls is defeated by bottlenecks due to the behaviours of managers—of an organization.

Frederick Taylor and the Scientific Management Theory

Frederick Winslow Taylor proposed a management approach that is also scientific in nature but unlike Fayol who looked at management from the director/manager or top to bottom point of view, Taylor focuses on the individual worker using the steel manufacturing industry to determine the cause of low and high productivity by factory production workers. To do this Taylor used the results from his finding on the individual worker as a benchmark to generalize and propose a style of managing upwards. Taylor considered the interest of workers to be equivalent to that of the employer. He showed recognition for the use of suggestion boxes in organizations and even in machine shops. Further, Taylor advocated that managers and employers should seek for the best wherever it may be found in the most cost effective manner. This idea suggests that a criteria or a benchmark should be set to attain best practices in organizations through the determination of appropriate parameters to evaluate current processes and procedures by finding or fashioning out better ways and methods of achieving requisite standards in line with industry best practices.

Process Design

Process design comprises of two equally important words that convey very deep meanings.

1.   Process

Process is the systematic way of doing or carrying out a task. A process can be regarded as a subset of design, that is, it is a design that gives birth to a process because without a design for achieving a thing, there can be no process. For instance, to produce a loaf of bread there is a process to be followed, getting the flour, kneading it, baking it etc. It is composed of a sub-process that must be performed before a task can be said to have been completed. For a process to be in place, the following are cardinal as they form an integral part of what a process essentially is.

a.   Ordering
Ordering is the requirement for things to be done in a pre-determined and organised manner.

b.   Purpose
To achieve a meaningful result in any given task, there is a need to know why it is necessary in the first place to even undertake any project, and how to ensure this is done in the manner prescribed.

c.   Rationale
Here the reason for putting in place a given process is first clarified to all that are required to work out the successful implementation of the process to achieve the same understanding and result.

d.   Roles
Roles signify the role to be played by parties pertinent to the achievement of objectives in terms of the responsibilities, motivation and the basis of assigning tasks related to the process.

e.   Structure
      Structures refer to how to achieve set goals and objectives.

2.   Design

A design is the artistic impression of an object or product. It is from a design that a process can emanate. For instance, an architect's drawing of a building is a design, so also is the work of the sculptor, fashion designer or even an accounting system. Designs are a necessary requirement before an end product can be created. To design anything requires research, lots of thinking on the object or product to be designed and what is to be modelled. Process design therefore, refers to the totality of techniques, systems, and impressions used to envision a task and the step by step procedural guide to ensure a successful outcome in the achievement of organizational goals and objectives.

Benchmarking

Benchmarking may be defined as the continuous measurement of a process, product, or service compared to those of the foremost competitors, industry leaders, or to similar activities in the organization in order to find and implement ways to improve it. It is one of the cardinal principles of both total quality management and continuous quality improvement. In addition, benchmarking may be regarded as the practice of being humble enough to admit that someone else is better at something and wise enough to try to learn how to match and even surpass that person at it.

•   Key steps to successful benchmarking

1.   Process recycling;
2.   Implementing and monitoring;

3.   Development of appropriate action plans;
4.   Revision of performance goals;
5.   Communication of results of findings;
6.   Projection or prediction of future performance gaps;
7.   Analysis of performance gaps;
8.   Collation of data;
9.   Clear identification of what to benchmark.

•   Importance of benchmarking

Benchmarking helps an organization to:

i)   Become more competitive by allowing the implemen-
      tation of proven practices and technology rather than
      evolutionary change.
ii)   Review its processes externally and internally rather
      than mainly internally.
iii) Make comparison with 'world class' organizations in-
      stead of local industry averages. Consequently, man-
      agement team can be motivated to strive for higher
      standards through creative innovation.
iv)   Enhance its performance rather than playing continu-
      ous 'catch up'.
v)   Focus on market reality by evaluating its performance
      objectively instead of relying on historical data or per-
      ception.
vi)   Focus on improving areas where real problems exist
      based on industry best practices rather than on small
      and easy to solve problems that have no impact on
      the performance of the organization.

•   Areas where Benchmarking should focus on:

Benchmarking becomes effective when:

i)   Attention is given to mapping and measuring an organization's processes through identification of key areas that are cost or resource consuming.
ii)   Comparison of an organizations processes with those of leading organizations that are say, 20%—30% more efficient is made.
iii) Organizations adapt practices from other organizations to suit their own and aim tc achieve an overall cost reduction of say, 25%.
iv)   Enablers found more effective at the leading organizations in terms of practices that are considered beneficial are used and implemented.

Thus, benchmarking produces the desired result when;

i)   An organization welcomes change.
ii)   Senior management 'buys in' to any good idea or suggestions or findings.
iii) All line managers participate ir organizational decisions and activities.
iv)   Adequate budget is made available to obtain the information required.
v)   Strategy of the organization aligns with the exercise and vice versa.
vi)   Reciprocal arrangemen⁻ with leading organizations is engaged in an open and forth rignt manner.

   •   Benchmarking fails when:

i)   Senior managers do not show enough commitment.
ii)   Line management fail to make or provide necessary inputs.
iii)   There are far too many expectations much too soon.
iv)   There is no clear definition of the role of each of the teams.

v)   Selected members for the project do not fit or are in-
      appropriate for the team.
vi)   Organization's strategic intent does not make provi-
      sions for the use of benchmarking nor does it encour-
      age its introduction.

CHAPTER 11
Total Quality Management & Six SIGMA

TQM is a form of management that is aimed at entrenching an awareness of quality in all managerial processes. It has been employed in almost all facets of human endeavors, in government, manufacturing and service industries, education etc. The goal is to ensure that every facet of work or production has a benchmark it must attain to be considered as sufficiently standardized in terms of the outcome of a process in comparison to others. Basically, there are three parties that seek satisfaction in the use of TQM, these are:

a.   The Client -the client is the center of attention. To ensure that he gets the benefit or receives the service that is courteous efficient and timely, his satisfaction and enjoyment of the services rendered is uppermost in the mind of the organization that uses the TQM.

b.   The Shareholders- reflected in the quality of returns they receive in terms of dividends declared at the end of a given period.

c.   The Employees- in terms of the quality of life they enjoy both in life and at work thereby giving the needed impetus to achieve the required success in production and service delivery at all times. Consequently, members of an organization are imbued with the philosophy of "doing it right the first time".

•   Origin of TQM

Total quality management is often traced to Armand Feigenbaum's book titled 'Total quality control' written in 1961 in which he dealt with management issues on quality control as they pertain to principles, practice and administration. Other contributors to this subject include Joseph Jurans, W. Edward Demings, US Naval Air Systems command and Japanese companies like NEC where its former CEO Koji Kaboyashi is reputed to be the first to use TQM as evidenced by a speech he delivered in 1974 when he was a recipient of Deming Prize. TQM is often referred to as total quality control (TQC) by the Japanese who regard management and control as synonymous terminologies.

•   Benefits of TQM

Following are the benefits derivable from the use of TQM.

i.   Under TQM organizational structures become more flexible and are able to respond and adapt to the changing needs of clients.

ii.   Systems and procedures are simplified to ensure better service delivery to clients.

iii.   TQM instills in the members of an organization a culture of excellence and prompt product and service delivery.

- Principle on Which TQM is Based

i.   Top Management Support

Without the support of tcp management there can be no TQM. Indeed, it is the management that initiates or sees the need for a quality assurance system. To do this, management needs to formulate a quality policy to guide it in its decision-making and implementation of the system to meet its needs and aspirations.

ii.   Quality Structure Plan

Quality has to be carefully planned, programmed and implemented. This should be the concern and responsibility of line and staff management.

iii.   Client Focus

Client focus is an approach that is geared towards measuring and improving client satisfaction levels. It is a concept that is directed at ensuring that only the client decides what quality is. This leads to detailed analyses of who the clients are, what their needs are, what features are required of the company's service, how clients and competitors rate the service, and how the company can ensure the satisfaction of its clients.

iv.   Training & Recognition

This could be looked at from the perspective of the need for frequent training of staff and management of an organization to make them relevant and more productive. There is also a need to motivate staff by putting in place a system of rewards for those that have performed their duties and assignments efficiently and exceptionally.

v.   Enhance Teamwork

Team work is the key to achieving cohesiveness. With-out this, there can be no common focus or aim as disor-derliness will be the order of the day and various segments of a job may end up not being effectively coordinated to enable achievement of the objectives of the firm or orga-nization. Thus, teamwork gives each individual a sense of self accomplishment for their contributions to the successful completion of a project or assignment.

vi.   Quality Assurance

For Innovation to take place, management is duty bound to ensure the proper application of TQM procedures and techniques, which in this instance may be classified into five categories namely:

•   Technology

Technology helps to increase efficiency in the work place as it enables the simplification of work processes and improves product outputs while at the same time helping to improve employees and staff effectiveness and productivity in terms of both output of product and services. To innovate, there is a need to develop and manage a more effective and up-to-date management information system, as well as the invention of new equipment and modification of ex-isting equipment to suit current operational needs.

•   Manpower Management

This deals with issues regarding human resource man-agement, as they are critical to ensuring that all main pro-cesses are carried out effectively and efficiently. Examples of these organizational processes include planning, product quality assurance as well as strategic and operational decision making mechanisms including budgetary control. Management is responsible for the formulation and implementation of a comprehensive training policy which addresses the needs of staff and management in the areas of enhancement of their knowledge and skills in specific fields, provision of recreational programs that help to develop mental and physical well—being, self-concept or self image, performance appraisal systems and acknowledgement of efforts and contribution of staff which engenders team spirit and development of work group.

•   Organizational Structure

When an appropriate organizational structure that suits a company is in place, it enables the organization to respond quickly in an effective and efficient manner to client needs and the achievement of corporate goals and objectives. Hence, the structure of an organization determines the style and quality of management systems, and channels of communication processes of information sharing. Innovations to structures in place essentially means that new units may be created and old ones eliminated including diversification in response to increasing client patronage and needs.

•   Work Environment

Work environment must be conducive to the kind of business a company or organization is engaged in. A conducive environment helps the organization innovate as the environment brings about a certain inexplicable sense of fulfillment that triggers off creativity among staff and management and the environment also gives the organization a good sense of belonging in the eyes of the general public thereby commanding respect in their estimation.

- Capital Equipments

These consist of items like buildings, plant and machinery, vehicles etc. The quality of production and services rendered by an organization may be affected by the availability or lack of these assets. Further, innovations in this regard includes the maintenance of all equipment, replacement of old and obsolete equipments and installation of multipurpose equipments and renovation of infrastructures and facilities.

Six sigma

The word sigma is a Greek term that is frequently used in mathematical calculations to measure standard deviation, which is a statistical way of describing the variations that exist in a set of data, groups of items or process. In other words, it is a measure of efficiency in the achievement of a goal or target needed for optimal performance of a firm or organization. Thus, the degree to which an organization meets set production and manufacturing goals and targets with insignificant amount of defects is directly proportional to the successful outcome the firm can achieve.

The higher the percentage achieved in carrying out its business by the timely delivery of what the client has ordered, the higher the calibration of the firm's efforts on the six sigma scale. For example, consider a fast food business that achieves a 70 percent timely delivery of client orders without- defects, such a firm could be said to have achieved a 4 sigma. Although a very high percentage, it is still less than the optimal level that can be achieved by the organization. To achieve a six sigma therefore, the organization or company must be working at full capacity, which means that it must utilize its resources of human, material and other inputs to their full potentials. Hence, it is only when a company or firm is able to meet its target or potential 99.9997 percent of the time can it be said to be operating at the level of a six sigma!

Six -sigma is therefore a quality improvement program that is designed to promote effective utilization of resources by a firm or organization, particularly those in process or manufacturing business. The reason for using six-sigma is to measure the quality of products and services to eliminate any defects as the organization seeks for near perfection in all its production processes. It is therefore a disciplined process or procedure for achieving the desired goal, target, or objective of a firm.

Much has been written about six sigma; Peter S. Pande and Lawrence Holpp in their book "What is six sigma?" give very clear explanations and guidance on the purpose and usefulness of six sigma. This concept which is usually traced to Motorola was later adopted by General Electric (GE) in 1995 and also recently propagated by Jack Welsh an ex CEO of the company.

• 	Benefits of Six-Sigma to a Business

The benefits of Six Sigma are obvious and include:

i. 	Helping to Improve Company and Operational Efficiency.

Which is its day to day operations by helping to eliminate unnecessary delays and bottle necks occasioned by a lack of goal or target consciousness by staff and management who do not understand the place and importance of the client who is not concerned with any operational difficulties being experienced by the organization as he is only interested in meeting his own needs. Consequently, to ensure that it stays in business the firm must factor in the needs of the client which includes timely and effective supply and delivery of his orders to enable him satisfy or enjoy his money's worth.

ii.   Helps to Raise Productivity.

Six-sigma helps to raise productivity as there is a set target of what must be produced. This puts token employers in the attitude that ensures the achievement of this target or quota of production on a daily basis. To raise productivity a firm needs to ensure that all its machinery and tools required to carry out production are functioning well. Further, the firm needs employees who are highly motivated to deliver on its promises to ensure that all the values of six sigma are achieved to a very high degree.

iii.   Helps to Lower Cost.

To lower cost means to eliminate inefficiencies in production. Cost reduction also necessitates the firm looking inwards at what causes wastages and seeking to remove or eliminate this. To lower cost also entails seeking sources for good but cheap materials required for production as well as exploring other sources through research and development.

iv.   Helps to Improve Design Processes

The very essence of six sigma is to improve a production process which therefore means that to use it; the firm will need to begin by taking a good look at its current processes to identify where it can make improvements. This will therefore determine the type of process design that meets the needs of the organization.

vi.   Helps to Ensure Timely Launch and Completion of Service.

Without timely delivery, a firm cannot be said to be operating at the level of six sigma, beccuse products that are not released or launched as scheduled could lose the "first mover" advantage as only organizations that are conscious of the importance of time can easily cash in on the lack of sense of proper timing and will by the organization to instill and deliver on promises made to clients.

vii.   Promotes and Builds Client Loyalty.

When a company is known to keep its promises to clients it shows that such a company has its clients uppermost in its plans. It also implies that a company realizes that the reason it is still in business is because its clients have kept it there and even helped to spread the word even though this can also be done through advertisements. By eliminating impediments to client satisfaction, the firm ensures that it keeps the loyalty of the client by satisfying and always being in touch and seeking to find ways and products that will meet his needs at the prices he can afford for the company's service.

viii.   Helps to Develop Leadership Potentials in Management and Staff of an organization.

When people interact whether at home or at work or wherever they learn by interactions, six sigma raises the level of thinking of all that are concernec with achieving set goals and targets which makes for eff ciency and increase in the abilities of the management ard staff of the organization. The mere fact that objectives and targets are being met and even surpassed pre-supposes that everyone in the organization is learning something worthwhile which can be translated into leadership quality because when the stakes are high, those concerned have learned one of the greatest facts of life; that there should be no excuse for failure as what is worth doing at all is worth doing well!

Chapter 12
Strategic Planning for Consulting Firms

A strategy is a plan of action management takes in order to achieve its desired goals, policies and objectives. The word strategy was originally coined from a Greek word 'Strategia' which means 'Generalship', obviously referring to the military's maneuvering of troops into positions in preparation to engage the enemy in a battle.

In his book, *Strategic Planning*, George Steiner, a professor of management and one of the founders of *The California Management, provides some definitions of* strategy:

- Strategy is that which top management does that is of great importance to an organization.
- Strategy refers to basic directional decisions, that is, to purposes and missions.
- Strategy consists of the important actions necessary to realize these directions.
- Strategy answers the question: What should the organization be doing?
- Strategy answers the question: What are the ends we seek and how should we achieve them?

Further, since the word strategy was derived from the word "Generalship", a number of issues are involved in making strategies, some of these include that:

i.   Being a 'General' pre-supposes that a soldier having risen through the ranks has had adequate and proper training in leadership and direction of a military command or formation;

ii.   To maneuver the troops successfully, the soldier must have imbibed the necessary knowledge and tactics to be able to make decisions on the appropriate measure to take when faced with challenges in a war situation;

iii.   There is a need for proper planning in readiness for battle;

iv.   There is an enemy who has a measure of intelligence about us that must only be engaged after a proper assessment of our own strengths and weaknesses as well as that of the enemy, to enable the appropriate strategy for overcoming him (the enemy) to be put in place.

Why Strategy is important

i.   To have a successful outcome at the end of any given operation or battle;

ii.   To make well informed decisions;

iii.   To assess own strengths and weaknesses;

iv.   To assess the strengths and weaknesses of competitors;

v.   To determine opportunities as well as threats and how to overcome them;

vi.   To project an organization's performance in relation to that of its competitors.

Qualities of a product Strategy

I.   A product strategy achieves desired results;

II.   A product strategy is one that has been carefully planned and thoroughly investigated that leads to a successful conclusion, on which basis a decision is then taken for appropriate action;

III.   A product strategy provides leadership and direction for an organization or corporation;

IV.   A product strategy projects into the future of an organization and helps to fashion ways to achieve desired goals and objectives in the midst of competitors.

Strategic Management (Organization Strategy)

Strategic management is the process of specifying, and developing policies and plans for the smooth running of an organization. It is the highest form of responsibility in the organization and is usually the exclusive preserve of the chief executive officer (CEO) who is ultimately responsible for the successful implementation, allocation and commitment of all required resources to ensure that desired outcome is achieved. Strategic management is a combination of strategy formulation and implementation. Strategy formulation involves an analysis of competitors, situations, and self- evaluation as well as the analysis of the micro and macro environment which is also closely related to the organization's strategic plan.

Strategic implementation on the other hand deals with issues that border on the proper application of plans in terms of resource allocation, process monitoring, training and welfare issues, evaluation of product and organizational performance against plans for the purpose of understanding the reasons for variances.

Consequently, an organization's strategy is an integral part of its strategic plan. It is essentially a blue print of how it intends to achieve the aims, goals and objectives for which it was established. As a consultant, your organization's strategy should consider questions on:

a.   Age and demography with a view to determining who your likely clients are, and how to meet their needs;

b.   The places of abode of likely client that is, where do they reside? In the cities, ghettos or high—brow areas or villages?

c.   Most effective method of advertisement to reach your target market such as, bill-boards, radio, television, pamphlets etc;

d.   Service differentiation- how to provide the service that your competitors cannot ordinarily make available at the moment or even if they do how your organization can add value to its products and services through differentiation?

e.   Determination of your organization's strengths, weaknesses, opportunity and threats (SWOT) to ensure its survival and success.

Strategic Planning

A strategic plan sets out the step by step method(s) to be applied by an organization in order to reach its goals. Remember, we defined strategy as a plan of action utilized for the purpose of achieving an organization's ends and means. Likewise, a strategic plan is a management tool used to improve performance. When a plan is in place, all the stakeholders will have a sense of duty and commitment to ensure its actualization. Thus, a strategic plan gives direction and focus to a company or business and helps to properly prioritize and efficiently allocate resources.

The Contents of a Strategic Plan

Following are the usual contents of a strategic plan.

i.   Vision statement

A vision statement defines where an organization intends to be in the future. It paints an optimistic picture to propel and help the achievement of planned and desired results.

ii.   Mission statement

A mission statement is a statement of purpose, goals and priorities of a company or organization. It tells where the organization is going now. It is advisable to keep mission statements as simple and short as possible. Mission statements should be about the satisfaction of the client's first before any other priority.

i.   Mandate

A mandate is an authority to carry out a given assignment or plan on behalf of an organization. A mandate gives the necessary backing to the executor of a strategic organization plan or objective.

ii.   Strategic drivers

These come from the statement of purpose of an organization. Drivers propel an organization towards achieving the reason for coming into existence. An example of drivers is the demographic and age distribution of likely user's of the organization's services for the purpose of meeting their needs.

iii.   Value statements

A value statement is a declaration of shared values around which workers communities and organization's can rally round. Value statements create a sense of togetherness within an organization. Examples of these kinds of statements include:
a.   Efficiency and effectiveness;

b.   Provision of quality and innovative service;
c.   Ensuring that employees are adequately motivated;
d.   Performance metrics.

These all set out to establish benchmarks for determining the performance of an organization holistically in relation to its mission, service quality, processes etc. it seeks to review the organizations performance through the employment of total quality management techniques among others.

Scope of Strategic Planning

The term scope is used in reference to the degree of strategic planning required to improve or revive an organization to the extent that it can conveniently achieve its goals and objectives, depending on the ability to provide answers to the following pertinent questions.

i.   How competent are board members? Because the more competent a board is the more likely it is to appreciate the importance of having a well thought out strategic plan. Conversely, it is also very likely that an incompetent board may not see the need for a thorough and comprehensive plan.

ii.   Is the organization having problems? An organization in crisis will need to have its plans reworked if it already has a plan in place to enable it discover areas where management has acted without recourse to the existing strategic plans or changing plans that are clearly not bringing the desired results.

iii.   What is the stage of development of the organization? Is it a new organization just starting, or, is it a franchise that has only changed ownership? That is, the stage of development of the organization plays a crucial role in determining the depth of strategic plan that will be required to turn a failing organization around or to put in place an adequate strategic organization plan. Again, the size of the organization whether small, medium, large or even complex is important in determining the type of plans required to turn its fortunes around.

iv.   How diverse are the stakeholders? Stakeholders are people who have vested interest in the performance or otherwise of a given project, investment or organization. The usual stakeholders for any organization are government and its institutions, researchers, students, employees, shareholders and the general public etc. These also influence the extent of a strategic organization plan.

v.   What is the culture of the organization? Any organization that does not have a culture of planning obviously may be heading for failure. Plans are a necessary part of an organization and corporate strategy and should not be dispensed with nor made light of.

Levels of Strategy

a.   Organization Unit Level Strategy

A unit level strategy adopts a separate plan of attack for each profit center of an organization. As a result, specific plans are tailored to promoting the success of individual products and services to make them have a competitive advantage in the market.

b.   Corporate Strategy

Corporate strategy is the level of strategy responsible for the overall direction a business will take in regards to its actions and plans. In this plan is the decision on which market, region or service industry to compete in, what amount of resources, staffing, cash equipment etc. to commit or deploy to ensure that goals and targets are achieved. Equally important is the management style to be adopted for large organizations in terms of its hierarchical structure, whether through direct corporate intervention (centralization) or through persuasion (decentralization). In order words, corporate strategy takes care of the bigger picture as it covers every conceivable area of an organization's enterprise.

c.   Functional Level Strategy

A functional level strategy is concerned with the operational effectiveness of all the processes and value chain of an organization. A process may be defined as a high level model employed by an organization to create value for its clients in relation to products and services to meet their needs. Value chain on the other hand is also a high level model that explains how an organization receives raw materials, adds value to it, through all kinds of processes leading to finished products and services for the benefits of its clients among others.

The Seven 'S' Models of Strategy

Thomas J. Peters of 'In Search of Excellence Fame' in conjunction with Robert H. Waterman and Julien .R; made a bold attempt at providing a structure for companies and organizations for the purpose of having a holistic view and a better understanding of the workings of an organization and its ability to be competitive and to adopt appropriate strategies for its products and services.

i.   Skills are an essential ingredient in the success or otherwise of an organization, the more skillful its staff, the more competent the organization will become and consequently better able to compete. Skills range from the ability to speak a foreign language, to; research and development, client service supports etc.

ii.   Staff implies care and attention to staffing and welfare matters. An organization's workforce is important to its development, hence the need to consider adequate motivation in terms of training, wages etc. Many companies are often guilty of neglecting this key area of overall organization success.

iii.   Strategy as earlier discussed is the plans and actions organization applies to ensure its pride of place in the market it chooses to operate in.

iv.   Structure; the structure of an organization determines how it is going to be managed and it prescribes what the focus of the organization will be. Consequently, an organization's structure depends on its orienta-tion whether it would be more responsive to its clients in which case it would adopt a client structure which then ensures that all organization skills are channeled towards achieving desired objectives or a functional structure in line with what it seeks to achieve in the short and long-term. In a functional structure, jobs and activities are grouped together, the goal of this form is to break or divide work into departments, e.g. finance, manufacturing, sales etc.

v.   A system is the process and method of information gathering adopted by an organization to achieve its ends and means. The sum total of these processes and methods applied in running and resolving simple and complex problems is what is referred to as systems. This includes the management acccunting system, mar-keting research systems among others.

vi.   Style or culture connotes a pattern of behavior, com-portment, reasoning, thoughts or symbols that have come to be associated with an organization as a result of its consistent and continual use over a long period of time.

vii.   Shared values or super ordinate goals. An example of this could be 'to be forward looking and innovative'. These are the all-consuming and passionate ideas held by members and staff of an organization on which products and services are built.

Pure Types of Strategies

Pure strategies may be categorized into three, namely, defenders, prospectors, and analyzers. The use of the word 'Pure' is to further give impetus to the term strategy and because it demonstrates the utility and applicability and general strategy orientation at the organization level and the strategic orientation level of subsidiaries since the main reason for any foreign direct investment is to:
a.   To develop new markets;
b.   To maintain current market position;
c.   To maintain market position as well as expand into new territories and markets.

1.   Defender

From the analysis given above it is evident that the defender does everything within its powers to maintain its market position through market research, exceeding client expectations and training of staff to meet competitive challenges faced by the organization. They also expect that staff will stay and grow with the organization for a long time. Defenders create a safe and secure share of the market and also make moderate allowances for growth and expansion.

2.   Prospectors

Prospectors on the other hand are forever seeking greener pastures for themselves as they are wont to seek out new organizations and expansion opportunities for their organizations. They are therefore characterized by rapid growth deployment and redeployment of resources on a continuous basis. In addition, they invest heavily in entrepreneurially skilled staffs that are adept at recognizing investment opportunities no matter where they may be found.

3.   Analyzers

Here, management believes that given the opportunity it can compete both at the early stages of a products
development as well as in the future. This belief is borne by
the fact that it continually seeks to upgrade technical abilities as well as managerial abilities in line with its developmental goals and aspirations. The lesson therefore is that
strategy is a conscious effort to position an organization to
compete favorably in any environment it operates in.

Chapter 13
Proposals: Stating Terms and Conditions of the consulting engagement

A proposal is a document or letter written to a client stating the terms and conditions of the assignment to be carried out in favour of the client and as agreed with him during the interview.

Why a Proposal is Necessary

The main reason for writing a proposal is to:

i.   Form the basis for a contract

A well written proposal only needs minor adjustment to become a contract. In order words the contents of a proposal are the inputs for a contract as a contract is normally written from the agreement reached during the interview.

ii.   To conclude or finalize the terms of agreement

To do this, the consultant should ensure that he writes the proposal in a manner that enables him seal the deal as it were. The client may request for a proposal inspite of having agreed to the terms of the proposal verbally.

iii.   To document the task to be carried out

A written proposal enables the consultant put in black and white the services to be performed or carried out by him. It helps to clear all grey areas with the client so that a mis-understanding on the nature and extent of work to be done is made very clear from the onset.

iv.   To agree on the duration of the assignment

The timeframe within which the task is to be performed is very crucial to a project as any thing to the contrary may render the project obsolete and irrelevant to the objective of the assignment. An example is considering the implication for arriving at an examination hall at the end of the examination when other students must have finished taking the test. Further, the time sequence of events for the project is important as the client may be desirous of having a certain amount of information before the project is over and done with.

v.   To set out the fees to be paid by the client

The fees to be received during and after the engagement should be communicated in the proposal even though it may have been agreed verbally with the client. This helps to avoid problems later.

Structure of a Good Proposal

An ideal proposal is one that is written in a:

a)   Clear and logical manner in terms of structure;

b)   Friendly and professional style;

c) Way that anything that has not been agreed upon with the client is not included no matter how tempting this may be.

d) Manner that the contents of the proposal have be confirmed and re-confirmed with the client before submission even if it is on the telephone where the client cannot be easily recched. This helps to ensure that all matters included in the proposal are the very same things that the client wants to be done.

Further, a good proposal is one that has an:

1. Introduction or Opening

This re-iterates the ideas for the project that were discussed during the initial interview.

2. Background Information

The background information tells how the project came about and the general assumptions that have been made about the project by the client. It also forms an opinion on whether his assumptions are right or wrong which should be communicated in a tactful way. Shou d the client insist on the use his assumptions rather than that of the consultant, he (the consultant) has the option to either accept or reject the assignment if he is not comfortab e working with the client's assumptions.

3. Purpose or Objective

A good proposal should state the purpose or objective to be achieved by the engagement as agreed with the client. This could mean:

a)   Developing turnover targets for the client within a pe-
     riod of say, 6 months to one year
b)   Making recommendations on the adequacy or oth-
     erwise of the present staffing level to enable achieve-
     ment of sales targets.

c)   Establishing or identifying new markets for the client's
     service.

4.   Research Methodology

This refers to the method to be used among all other
options and stating why a particular method was chosen.
A consultant should endeavour to communicate and educate his client on the strengths and weaknesses of the option chosen against the other alternative methods as well
as tell them what those other alternatives are.

5.   Areas of Potential Problems

Further, he should inform the client about the areas
where he may likely have problems in the course of the assignment. In other words, he should help them appreciate
the solutions he is proposing to solve the problem at hand
and also documenting them.

6.   Flow Charts

Flow charts are series of symbols that are interconnected and show the sequences and progression of work to be
done in their order. Flow charts are used by auditing firms
and by consultants handling complex assignments for large
organizations. An example of flow chart is Performance
Evaluation and Review Technique (PERT).

7.   End or Finished Service

Very often clients may be eager to have a feel of what the likely outcome of a project would be. This he does by requesting information about the project on the form or shape the final report will take such as in photographic, graphical or in a documentary form etc. and in what quantity. The idea is to be able to project what the end service will be and to whom they are to be distributed such as to members of the board of directors and other key members of staff. The date of delivery is also important.

8.   Fees

The amount to be paid by the client during and after the completion of the assignment should be communicated to the client. The number of instalments should also be agreed upon with him.

How to convert a proposal into a contract

A proposal when properly written as said earlier forms the basis for a contract. The difference between the two is that whereas the former is made to seal a deal after the initial interview, the latter is an appendage of signatures to an already sealed deal. In other words, a proposal may be turned into a contract when a provision is made for the signatures of the client if he agrees with the terms proposed by him. In France and Belgium it is customary to have a client endorse in his own hand writing that he accepts by writing "Bon Pour Accord", meaning that he agrees to the terms being proposed.

Accountants

Accountants can be very useful to a consulting practice regardless of its size because apart from helping to guide a business in keeping proper records to enable it know when it is making a profit or a loss, they prove invaluable in the area of tax planning whereby they help a business know what to avoid when paying taxes in order to reduce the amount of taxes to be paid to revenue authorities. What the accountant does to help is to limit the amount to be paid when preparing tax returns by deducting or reducing operating expenses and similar expenses from the gross profit to arrive at the net profit on which taxes are computed.

In addition, accountants are useful in that they help a business understand and keep abreast with tax laws of the country it operates in, thereby helping to certify the business free from tax evasion by the relevant tax authorities. I recommend using the services of professionally qualified accountants but they however will charge a moderate fee for their services.

What is gross profit?

Another term for gross profit is trading profit which is arrived at after the cost of goods sold (COGS) is deducted from sales or turnover.

Attorneys

Attorneys like the accountant are very useful to a consulting practice as they help with firming up legal documents. Care should be taken however, on how their services are used since they basically charge by the hour for services rendered. It is therefore wise to see if some of the questions to be asked the attorney could be researched before meeting with them.

In addition, certain items such as contract documents, agreements etc. can be easily found or downloaded from the internet and adapted to specific situations. In any case, it is advisable to seek out an attorney to guide or to look at a document introspectively to ensure that all loose ends have been properly tied together to avoid any unforeseen litigations as a result of non performance of certain aspects or clauses in the contract.

Chapter 14
Consulting Contract

A contract is a legally binding exchange of promises between two parties that the law will enforce. Contracts can come in several forms, e.g.

a.   Oral or written;
b.   Implied or expressed;
c.   Legally enforceable or otherwise.

Strong contracts for the purpose of enforcement have:

a.   An offer;
b.   An Acceptance;
c.   A Consideration for the exchange;
e.   Clearly set out the terms of the agreement without ambiguity;
f.   To be signed by the involved parties having proper capacity to enter into the contract.

Weak contracts on the other hand include those made by verbal agreements or those made but which are in direct conflict or violation with the state or federal laws. Majority of contracts made by individuals and parties to a contract are Oral contracts, For example, Mr. A agrees to give a reward to Mr. B, if he carries out his wishes. This exists in a father and son relationships where the father could promise a vacation to an exotic beach or the purchase of an item, say a car if the son passes his examination with flying colours.

Implied contracts occur when one takes a loan, for instance, it is implied that he is to pay back the loan in installments together with any interest and late payment fees. Other contracts could be implied as well as oral, for example, when food is ordered from an eatery, it is implied that the person making the order will pay for it. This is so because the basic elements of a contract such as an offer, acceptance, and consideration for the offer are all implied.

Offer and acceptance are pertinent since it is necessary to sound the minds of the parties involved to ensure that they are all in the right frame of mind or disposition required to append their signatures to the contract. Contracts are accordingly expected to have Considerations either in monetary terms or otherwise built into them to be enforceable. The law requires that the Consideration should be adequate to prevent injustice. To be enforceable therefore, parties to a contract must intend for it to be, otherwise it will be unenforceable, e.g. the agreement between father and son if he passes his examinations with flying colours would ordinarily be unenforceable by law since it was not intended to be so from the outset.

Further, the following can also render a contract unenforceable:

i.   Irregularities on the face of the contract;
ii.   If one of the parties has diminished capacity such as being underage or mentally retarded;
iii.   Fraud or misrepresentation by any of the parties to the contract.

Contract risks are therefore financing risks as well as risks associated with clients and vendors. Liabilities that are a result of contract risks can be limited to the contract itself.

Why a consulting contract is necessary

A consulting contract is necessary to ensure that a common understanding is achievec with the client concerning the extent of work that is required to be carried out since the end expectation is that the client should be happy with the services being rendered by the consultant and which could lead to other jobs and referrals by the client to others.

Further, a consulting contract is necessary because of the financial obligations involved to avoid any ambiguities especially in the event that things do not turn out as planned and the need to sue arises because of the need to be paid for work done.

Choosing the form of contract to adopt

While it is possible to develop ones own contract to be employed in every contractual situation with minor amendments with regards to amount of compensation, duration of engagement, services, and information on one's client etc. it is advisable to seek the advice of an attorney to do this. Of- course not necessarily all aspects of the contract to avoid huge cost or charges by the attorney. However, it may be better to develop relevant aspects of the contract by oneself.

On the other hand the client may already have a contract in hand which could be keyed into. This type of situation is common with large corporations. Although corporations are often fair with their terms cf the contract, nevertheless, it is the responsibility of the consultant to study the terms of such contracts before agreeing to it. In addition, the attorney should also study the contract to enable him iron out any grey areas with the client.

How to enter into a contractual obligation

i.   formal contract

A formal contract is a written agreement describing what each party must do. It spells out each party's obligation and helps to prevent any mis-understanding in the future regarding the work to be done and the fees to be paid.

ii.   Letter contract

Letter contracts contain all the elements to a contract but differ from a formal contract in style, language and certain aspects of a formal contract. As such they are simple letters written from a proposal to carry out a consulting assignment.

iii.   Order agreement

Order agreement contracts are used for purchasing consultancy services that span a period or length of time. The idea behind this method of contract obligation is to commit the consultant and the client to the terms of the contract prior to authorizing the work to be done. Consequently, the number of hours to be spent on the job, the amount to be paid, when to begin the execution of the contract (prerogative of the client), etc. is clearly set out in the order agreement. However, the client may wish to reserve the right to use the services or not.

iv.   Purchase order

A purchase order contract is typical of large corporations and is an internal form used for authorizing a job and to also present the bill for work done. The reason for using this method is to cut time wastages and formal contract procedures that may involve a client's legal department seeking to carry out their own end of the contract to the letter before work can commence. To safeguard company funds and assets, management may decide to put a ceiling on the amount at which a purchase order contract may be awarded.

v.   Verbal Contracts

A verbal contract is a word of mouth contract to carry out a consulting assignment. Since this is not an ideal way to carry out a contract, my advise to a consultant is to insist on collecting a mobilisation or part payment as well as ensuring that grey areas have been ironed out with the client before beginning the job.

Main types of contracts in consulting

i.   Fixed price contracts

A fixed price contract is one that the amount for carrying out the work is fixed before the commencement. In order words a consultant is required to estimate the cost at which he wishes to carry out the requested work and it is on the basis of his quotation subject to agreement by the client that he begins the work. In some instances, the amount quoted for the job may eventually turn out to be more or less than the cost of carrying out the work. This s why he is advised to take extra precaution to be conversant with the pricing of the work to be done so that he does not suffer a loss at the end of the day as a result of understating the price.

ii.   Cost contracts

Here the actual amount spent in carrying out the work or assignment is the amount that will be paid by the client. It is a time based contract and therefore all associated expenses are added to the cost of services being offered by the consultant. It is not unusual to find that clients object to cost based contracts and would rather prefer to know the price and agree before commencing the work, i.e. a fixed cost contract. Whichever is the choice of the client; the consultant should not lose sleep over the client's preferences but ensure that he is able to make a reasonable estimation of the cost involved so that he does not experience a loss after completing the work given to him.

Further, cost contracts may be categorised into:

a)   Cost plus fixed fee and

Here, a consultant receives the total cost of the contract plus a fixed amount as agreed by both parties.

b)   Cost plus incentive

In this method, a consultant is paid the cost plus a variable incentive based on different levels of performance of the contract.

In all, both methods are frequently used by government agencies for project research and development.

iii.   Performance contracts

A performance contract is one in which payment for services rendered to a client are based on actual performance. For instance, when recruitment agencies are given the task of filling available vacancies for a client, under a pure performance contract, they only get paid when their recommended candidate gets the job. In other words, they get nothing if their candidate does not get hired. Further, a performance contract may be based on measurable factors such as an increase or decrease in sales etc.

My advice is to beware of performance contracts that are tied to profit. The reason is because what is profit in real accounting terms differ because companies are able to understate their profits with the help of a good accountant who understands tax planning, thereby avoiding or helping to reduce the amount left as profits for an organization. Further, my counsel is for the consultant to take the initiative in closing the deal by determining what price quotation he wants for the work to be done, e.g. carrying out a marketing campaign. He may himself elect not to get paid if a certain percentage of improvement is not recorded in the sales or turnover of a company's products or services after a certain period. If on the other hand, the reverse is the case, i.e. if the company does record an appreciable level of growth equalling say, 30% as forecast by the consultant, then the company is duty bound to pay the amount of say, $10,000.00 demanded by him.

iv.   Incentive contract

Like the performance contract, an incentive contract is also based on performance or a combination of fixed-price or cost contract if certain goals or objectives are met. My advise is to ensure that the target set is realistic and acceptable and also being aware that the objective should be the nurturing of a long term business relationship with the client. Examples of this kind of contract include the promise of an additional reward if certain sales are made over and above a certain number, e.g. undertaking to pay Mr. X $30

for every student in excess of the projected enrolment fig-
ure in a school.

Basic elements required in any contract

The following elements are required in every contract.

i.   Who

a)   Who the client is;
b)   Who the consultant is;
c)   Who the other parties involved in the project are.

ii.   what

What the nature of service to be rendered is.

iii.   where

a)   Where the service is to be provided;
b)   Where the consultant's official address is situated;
c)   Where the client's business is situated;
d)   Where other special locations are situated.

iv.   when

When seeks to make clear the timing of the execution
of the service and the associated payments.

v.   How much

How much implies knowledge of the amount of compensation to be made for the services rendered.

In addition to the above requirements, a consultant will
do well to ensure that issues covering patent rights, insur-

ance coverage, confidentiality, competitive restrictions etc. are dealt with and agreed upon before commencing or signing the contract agreement.

Chapter 15
Make Professional Presentations & Communicate Effectively

What should a consultan⁻ be talking about all the time? Actually, nothing but business! In other words, he should be consumed with passion for what he does and what he can offer his clients. In addition, he is required to treat business with dispatch; with speed by being up and doing, ready from day one (and at all times) to attend to the needs of his clientele.

He should literally talk the talk!

By watching what he says;
How he says it;
When he says it;
Where he says it; and
Why he says what he says.

In the US it is called the *elevator speech*, which simply means that in seeking to promote his business or increase his clientele base, a consultant should be ready *at all times* with a brief outline of what he does (since he does not know whom he might meet at any point in time) and should be able to deliver his speech within 20 to 30 seconds in about a hundred words.

Timothy R.V Foster, in his book *How to succeed as an independent consultant* opines that a consultant's (elevator) speech should punctuate and capture in succinct terms the following:

a)   His target market;

b)   Product solution;

c)   What the product does;

d)   The derivable benefits from the use of the service;

e)   What differentiates his product solutions from those of his competitors.

Further, he counsels that in describing what he does, a consultant should place importance on the end results rather than the process he goes through to achieve his objectives, such as:

i.   Helping clients to be more result oriented in the delivery of client satisfaction, rather than providing client's with motivational training packages.

ii.   Developing and implementing local communication networks in a way that puts the mind of the client to rest rather than the review and specification of computer packages.

Why Communication is important to an organization

A good system of communication is cardinal to the survival of any organization as it helps to:

a)   Facilitate the sales of products and services.

b)   Maintain all tiers of Government i.e (local state and Federal Government) by attracting the right amount of investments and capital required for growing and meeting the needs for infrastructure developments at these various levels to enable them meet the challenges they face.

c)   improve the productivity of workers of an organization.

The effects of an inefficient system of communication are obvious as more organizations become vulnerable to a heightened level of pressure from Government, community groups, the press as well as consumers.

What is a presentation?

A presentation is a lecture or speech that is set forth for an audience, in this case the client. A consultant's success in any engagement is to a large extent dependent on carrying out the assignment professionally as well as making effective and informative presentations of the result of the work to the client.

The purpose of Presentations

The objective of any presentation is to inform the client about the findings or result of the engagement as well as making recommendations and confirming to the client that the task has been completed. This action may lead the client to retain the services of the consultant and to also recommend him to other prospective clients.

Further, it is a consultant's responsibility to seek out ways and means for getting his client to understand the recommendations he has put forward. It is only by doing this that he will be encouraged to see the recommendations as real solutions to the problems he seeks to solve. Accordingly, the consultant should endeavour to explain to the client the methods he has adopted to reach the conclusions and why he has chosen a particular method.

In addition, clients may wish to know the problems encountered in the course of the engagement and how the consultant was able to go around these problems. Further, if he has made basic assumptions as a result of a lack of information on certain areas of the assignment, clients want to know what these assumptions are and how they were reached.

In a nutshell, the client is interested in knowing in a concise manner the methodology and all that is entailed in reaching the recommendation and confirmation of a good work done by a consultant. Consequently, a consultant should not forget to include any contract changes agreed upon with the client.

Keys to Effective Presentation

1.   Enthusiasm

Enthusiasm is a great excitement for or interest in a subject or cause. It is that element that keeps one going even when there is a lack of interest or excitement at doing something or carrying out an assignment. Enthusiasm is very important to the accomplishment of any worthwhile task or assignment. It may be regarded as the most important element in making a product presentation because an enthusiastic person or personality has the innate tendency and ability to affect and influence others to their way of thinking thereby helping to get the message across to the audience.

However, it may not be possible to always be enthusiastic at all times especially when the task at hand is one that a consultant is not comfortable with. In such instances he is advised to put on an enthusiastic attitude. In other words he should pretend to like and enjoy the task at hand for by so doing, it may well turn out that the assignment becomes one that he thoroughly enjoys doing. Consequently, an enthusiastic attitude will help deliver on promises to the client through an effective presentation.

2.   Professionalism

The American college dictionary provides the following regarding professionalism:

A profession is "a vocation *requiring* knowledge of some department of learning or science."
A professional is one who follows "an occupation as a means of livelihood or gain," or one who is "engaged in one of the *learned* professions."
Professionalism is exhibited by the "*professional character, spirit or methods*" or the "standing, practice, or methods of a professional as *distinguished from an amateur.*"
From the above, it is clear that a professional is that individual who is versed and well acquainted with his vocation or calling, one that can hold his own anywhere, any day, and anytime before the client or audience. A professional is expected to prepare well in advance before making a

presentation to the audience and must not leave things until the dying minutes before attempting to do them in a hurried manner.

In order words, he should be a professional to the core, in the way he carries himself, in dressing and general comportment as well as in ability. He must make sure that he has gone through the work to be presented to ensure that there are no grammatical mistakes or typographical errors because anything to the contrary will lead the client and audience to conclude that he is no professional after all.

3.   Organization

Proper organization of thought and ideas one wishes to pass across to the client or audience is very crucial and will determine one's effectiveness or otherwise. An un-organized presentation of ideas and thoughts will make a consultant vulnerable to his client and may cause him to lose confidence in him and his work. The fact of the engagement should therefore be presented with clarity in such a way that ideas put forth are logical and show:

i)   The origin of the consulting assignment and the problems that require solutions.

ii)   A statement of the purpose; goal; target: or objectives to be accomplished.

iii)   The method to be used in carrying out the task at hand as well as other methods that could have been adopted for the assignment but were rejected and the reason why they where not found suitable for resolving the issues at hand.

iv) The challenges or difficulties experienced during the engagement and how they were addressed.

v)   The outcome or results obtained from the assignment.

vi) Recommendations for the client on the types of actions to take to get the problems at hand solved.

4.   Practice

To practice a thing means to continually do such a thing until a level is reached where one is comfortable with it. It is often said that "practice makes perfect". This means that repetition of a thing leads to a level where one gains mastery of the work or object of attention or interest. Practice can be done in front of a mirror or before someone who could give an objective assessment of one's performance, or through live demonstration's before the actual day of the event. Some aids to effective practice include the use of 3- by -5 inch file cards or visual aids such as Microsoft PowerPoint to make presentations. Further, it is essential that while practicing, that time control as well as getting the facts across in a succinct manner should be the objective.

Too much detail may make an individual or consultant exceed the allotted time for the presentation thereby defeating the aim of the presentation which is to convince the client on the veracity of the solutions to the problem being put forward. In any case, the client may have other engagements to attend to which therefore necessitates doing a professional job within all the parameters that have been given to be adhered to.

4.   Visual aid

Visual aids are those objects that help to facilitate a better understanding and presentation. These come in different shapes and sizes and include:

i)   35mm slides

These are usually employed where presentations involving photographic details are to be made. They however are considered a pain in the neck where they fail to show the desired objects as envisaged or where the pictures being shown are turning the other way round, i.e. right side up or up side down as the case may be. In addition, there is the problem of waiting for a lead time, usually a week or two before they can be made ready for use.

ii)   Handouts

Handouts are hard copies of the detailed items or topics of discussion duly explained and expatiated upon by the consultant or someone making a presentation. Handouts are the most frequently used form of visual aids. They may also be regarded as the most effective since each participant in the audience is expected to be given a copy of the handout to enable them follow the presentation without difficulty. Handouts however, have drawbacks in that the audience may read ahead making them get ahead of what the presenter may intend to pass across in a special way. In addition, depending on the number of audience, it may involve a substantial amount to produce a copy of the handout for each participant on a piece of paper. Handouts may also be reproduced on a CD-ROM.

iii)   Overhead transparencies

These are used with overhead projectors and with an area of about the size of an A4 size paper or 9/ 11 inches which can be also be made on a computer or photocopier or printer. Transparencies are easier to use than slides or flip charts and can easily be carried around.

iv)   Black or white boards

The name above should not be taken as the only colour possible for writing or instructional boards as they may be green blue or whatever colour the producer's deems fit. These boards are used in conjunction with markers or felt pens of different colours to write on the boards as opposed to the use of chalk with all the noise and dust. Boards have the advantage of flexibility of use and changes to what has been written can be done on the spot as it commits no one until he has actually written something on the board.

In addition, boards and chalk presentations are inexpensive compared to electronic gadgets. A chalk presentation however, has a disadvantage in that it cannot be reproduced like handouts or 35mm transparencies and is time wasting as the audience may be idle while the presenter is writing on the board, which may lead to distractions especially where the hand writing of the person making the presentation is not legible enough.

v)   Computer Presentations

Computers may be used in making presentations through the use of Power Points and projectors. A lot of money can be saved from the use of these types of presentations since there may be no need for transparencies and for producing hard copies or handouts of what is to be presented. However, despite the advantages inherent in the use of computer presentations, it is still replete with disadvantages chief of which is the problem of moving these equipments from one place to the other and may also lead to distractions during demonstration as the participants may be fascinated by the neat noises and graphics.

vi)   Flip charts

These are large charts connected at the top which are flipped over when each page is done with. Flip charts have the advantage of not requiring the use of projectors. As a result of its size, they are sometimes difficult to transport and the hand writing may not be seen by some people in a large audience.

In summary, the following considerations should be made in choosing a visual aid.

a)   The slides, charts, transparencies etc. should not be overloaded with too much information at a time. Only the essential points that will enable the presenter remember the main points should be put on the slides, transparencies etc. anything to the contrary may end up getting the audience confused.

b)   The print or fonts of the visual aid should be large enough to be read by the audience.

c)   Ensuring that there is enough time between the time required to prepare the resource materials for the flip charts, transparencies and slides in order to correct possible typographical errors to leave a professional impression on the audience.

Dealing with Stage Fright

Stage fright is what every presenter experiences. However, it can be controlled and even overcome by:

i.   Rehearsals

Engaging in formal rehearsals is recommended for a consultant or anyone due to make a professional presentation in order to get a feedback from people on how well he has performed. The level or degree of performance will provide an indication or insight on how ready he is for the *actual* presentation.

ii.   Mental rehearsal or creative visualization

This method was popularized by a performance psychologist, Charles Garfield and William Cohen author of *How to make it Big as a Consultant* and Norman Vincent Peale in the book *The Power of Positive Thinking*. They opine that mental rehearsals or creative visualisation is the style adopted by top athletes to visualize successful outcomes and can also be used by any one desirous of success in any field of endeavour. Mental rehearsal therefore involves going over what one intends to present to an audience in such a way that in one's mind's eye one sees the hall, the audience, their favourable responses and everything connected to the event working out in the manner expected. As a result of the frequency of rehearsals, stage fright will eventually be put under control giving a feeling of confidence of a good hold on what one is to deliver.

In the same way, in making a presentation a consultant should also prepare by envisaging the kind of questions he may likely be asked by the audience. He should also prepare the answers to the questions in succinct terms sharp and straight to the point by avoiding overly long answers to questions by seeing himself answering the questions in the manner expected thereby providing the needed answers and by implication the required solution to the problems posed. In answering questions, he should apply tact by not getting into an argument with the client or audience, noting the adage that the client is always right, even when his solution or envisaged answer to a problem is clearly wrong.

Chapter 16
Marketing Products and Services

All co-ordinated efforts directed towards the attainment of corporate goals and objectives pertaining its products or services, consumers or clients, etc are referred to as marketing which also involves the exchange of goods and services. It has been defined by Kotler et al; as a social and managerial process by which individuals obtain what they need and want by creating and exchanging products or services and values with others.

This essentially reveals among others that:

i.   Marketing involves management and its processes;
ii.   It involves the exchange of goods and services;
iii. It involves people, product, pricing, and plans;
iv.   It involves the mutual satisfaction of needs and wants in the process of exchange of goods and services.

What Management is about

The term management means getting things done through other people. By the same token it involves organizing, planning, controlling and directing the affairs of a company especially as they pertain to its marketing efforts among others. It adopts a procedural approach to achieving its set goals and objectives. To be relevant marketing must ensure soundness and adequacy of plans directed towards the attainment of value from goods and services as well as being profitable to the company concerned. It should also monitor and control the outcomes of plans through proper organization, focus and effective direction of aims and objectives. This in effect will help ensure successful outcomes for the goods and services offered by the company.

Exchange of Goods and Services

The exchange of goods and services involves two or more parties having needs or wants coming together for the purpose of meeting these needs or objectives. Marketing is regarded as successful when parties fulfill their needs. In the ordinary sense of the word an exchange of this nature will involve a consideration in the form of services for money. When a service is exchanged for another service it is referred to as trade by 'barter'.

Though it needs to be mentioned that barter is a rather difficult way to exchange products or services as a person with a need for say, a loaf of bread who has a tuber of yam may find it difficult getting anyone with such a need for an exchange to take place. Another area of difficulty is the place of meeting of suppliers and buyers in barter system as there may be the barrier of distance and proximity to the service. Also to be considered is the issue of more suppliers and buyers as there may be more choices of services to pick from as the market expands from a single buyer and seller to multiple buyers and sellers.

To be worthwhile therefore, marketing should be directed towards meeting needs as opposed to making money out of the consumers or clients of a company. This helps in focusing all marketing efforts at meeting their needs which when done satisfactorily adds value as it ensures loyalty as well as profitability for the business. Accordingly, it would amount to an error on the part of the management of the company if its main aim for being in business or selling a service is to make money as this desire or goal may eventually be in conflict with the company's long term goal of consumer or client loyalty. Consequently, it stands to reason that all marketing efforts should be balanced in such a way that consumer or client needs and wants are made part and parcel of what is to be produced before engaging in any production efforts.

Relationship Marketing

The consumer is central to any marketing effort for the following reasons.

i.   He is the most important person in any business.

As highlighted above the client is the main reason for being in business in the first place. Whatever the business and regardless of the size of an organization, the target market is the consumer base. A company must consider its consumers' interest because they make or mar a business or its services.

Customers or clients are often said to be kings by companies that understand their significance; because such companies seek diligently to serve them in the sense that all efforts are targeted at ensuring that they derive the envisaged benefits from the use of its products and services. This has in-built advantages as clients can help spread the word when a product delivers on its promises thereby making it profitable in the long-run while building a long-term relationship with clients as they really add value to a company.

ii.   He pays the salaries and wages of the employees.

Without the client, a company cannot sell its products or services. Consequently, it stands to reason that a company is likely to eat into its capital if it does not sell its products or services at least to earn a measure of profits to be used in the settlement of its obligations to its employees among others. In fact there cannot be a job when there are no customers or clients. This is why the client is often regarded as the actual employer of a company's workers. This fact is often lost on management and staff of some companies as they treat the client with levity as if they are doing him a favour instead of coming to the realization that the client is the one actually doing the company a favour as he patronizes the business through the purchase and use of its products and services.

iii.   He is cardinal to the design of company's product and services.

What would be the use of creating or designing a service that would not at the end of the day be sought after by consumers? The obvious answer is, no benefits at all but rather loses and a waste of precious time, resources and efforts. This is why it is very crucial to have products or services designed to suit the needs of the customer or client after discussing, researching, identifying and ascertaining his needs before going ahead to produce. In reality the customer or client goes in search of derivable benefits from the use of a product rather than the product itself. It is therefore crucial and imperative for companies to understand this simple truth and align their strategies along these lines if they intend to influence consumers to buy their products or services and to also ensure loyalty to the company.

He also determines when a company is ready to take on newer and bigger challenges.

Consumer behaviours cre indicative of how a company's service is perceived. If they like it and their needs are met while using the service, they show it through loyalty to the company and its service. On the other hand if they are dissatisfied with the service or even the company, they may show this by patronizing close substitutes to meet their needs, as the client is only interested in having his needs met. This then gives us an irsight into why the client is a key determinant of the growth or otherwise of a company or business since his behaviour affects the fortunes of the company. When he buys or uses the services, the company profits and he the consumer has his needs met. If on the other hand the reverse is the case, it will not augur well for the company and its products or services.

Growing Products/ services and creating More Business

A company desirous to increase patronage of its products and services will do well to heed the following advice.

i)   Create own niche market

The key to niche marketing is to find an area where needs are not been currently met by other suppliers or companies and tailor products and services to meet identified needs. By creating a niche a company can become the clear leader in an area of business and therefore the authority in that line as it will have an edge over competitors. Being the leader makes the company a rallying point in the industry, as it will be called upon to help build the industry by encouraging others to develop products and services that are complementary.

ii)   Create the right perception.

In order to grow its products or services a company or organization should make a deliberate effort to be seen and regarded in the way it desires to be perceived. This means that it should spend time positioning its business, products and services. Positioning entails creating the image one wants for one's company and its services in the minds and perception of the clients. This has the added advantage of guaranteeing the long-term existence of a company when it is done right as perception plays a major role in the way consumers patronize a company.

iii) Customize Service

Having identified a niche, a company can create products or services that the consumer or client can have, when he wants it, where, how, and in the right quality and quantity that he wants. This is what mass customization is all about and has been made easier by the advent of techno-logical breakthrough in this area. To succeed, there needs to be a relationship already in existence with clients as it is taken as given that it already exists without which the need or use for mass customization will be defeated.

Focusing on the Intangibles

Marketing efforts should be focused on those benefits that cannot be seen or touched. These are quality, dura-bility, reliability, and client orientation. This is pertinent if a company is to differentiate its services among competing alternatives.

Further, a company that seeks to retain its clients must promptly look into their complaints and grievances to prevent them from switching over to competitors. This can be done in the following ways:

a). Respecting the right of the client to express his frustrations regarding the treatments he or she has received from the people and staff of the company.

b). Addressing the issues raised by the client promptly and with dispatch. This should be done only after he has finished laying down his complaints. The company should take the lead by requesting politely what better ways he could be better served.

c). Following up the client to ensure that the issues raised have been resolved to his satisfaction.

d). Trying to win back lost clients by improving its product and services in such a way that they can be convinced to again patronize the company and not their competitors. Losing a client means losing a potential stream of income derivable from sales of a product or service to a satisfied client. This should not be taken lightly as the multiplier effects of lost clients eventually culminate into losses of potential revenues for the company.

e). A company must also realize that not all clients will express their grievances to them. As such reasonable care must be taken to ensure that:

i.   Employees are respectful and courteous to them and the company is operating in such a way that its products and services are among the best in the industry in terms of fast, efficient and qualitative delivery.

ii.   The appearance of company facilities usually convey
       messages to clients in the sense that an untidy or un-
       kempt environment and broken down facilities send
       the wrong signal to clients and therefore does not show
       pride in the business by its owners and management.

Chapter 17
The Concept of Marketing Mix

The four 4p's refer to marketing decisions also known as marketing mix, a term made popular by the work of Neil H. Borden in his article of 1964, *The concept of marketing mix* based on a description of the work of a marketing manager as a "mixer of ingredients" such as planning, pricing, branding, distribution channels, personal selling, advertising etc. by James Culliton, which was later summarised into the 4p's of marketing by E. Jerome McCharty which are discussed below.

a.   Products and Services

A product can be tang'ble or intangible and it is the principal activity and reason a company is in business because without a product there can be no company. In other words, a company is in business to provide products and or services to its clients based on their needs and wants having in mind the necessary required specification of the product and or services with inputs from the client. Apart from the product themselves, services also include the warranties, guarantees and after sales service supports.

b.   Place or (Placement)

Place refers to the location where products and services can be readily found by the client. A business should ensure that its products are strategically placed where they can easily be reached by the client. Here the channel of distribution is important as it will go a long way to determining how clients are supplied. This could either be through retail outlets or through the web or Internet or some other appropriate channels. Another means of reaching clients is by classifying them according to demographic, geographical, or industrial settings, which include the type of families, age group, business etc.

c.   Price

The price at which a product or service is sold is very important in determining the quantity that will be eventually sold to enable a company make a profit or to break even. There is no substitute to an appropriate pricing mechanism that ensures value for money, which is very crucial as a high price may scare clients away, and too low a price may result in the company not being able to make a profit. A key element of pricing worth knowing is that the price of a product or service need not be monetary as it could be determined by also taking due cognizance of the time, psychology, energy and attention expended in creating or producing the product or service.

Key pricing Strategies for your Consulting Firm

1.   Low price

A low price strategy is useful for penetrating a new market or for reaching new clientele since it will be lower than the prices set by already established competitors. Although advantageous in gaining clients by new entrants to the consulting business, it is nevertheless a tiring and time consuming strategy because of the need to work harder and for a longer time frame than already established counterparts for less amounts. In addition, a low price strategy may be responded to by these established consultants since they are likely to have the financial muscles to outwit the new entrant and so prevent him from taking away their clients.

Further, a low price strategy may carry the wrong message in the eyes of the client, in that he may associate low price to inability, inexperience or inefficiency or even outright cheapness. As a consultant just starting out, my advice is to ensure that you are aware of the advantages as well as the inherent disadvantages involved in using this strategy which also includes that it may be difficult to increase price at a later time.

2.   High price

A high is the exact opposite of the low a price strategy and suggests that a company is very sure of the kind of product or service it is offering to the market. Likewise, when it charges high prices for the services from the onset, it is actually taking a risk but one which may pay off if handled properly as clients perceive that it may be offering what the others are not. Consequently, the company is seen as efficient and competent and also able to deliver value for money. However, many new consultants are usually scared of charging high prices at the outset which may mean that they do not believe that they are worth the price being charged or that they are afraid that other consultants may undercut them to get the job.

3.   Meet-the -competition strategy

Here, a price that is comparable to what others in the market charge is chosen. A choice of this type of pricing strategy would necessarily mean ensuring that additional services are provided for clients along with the service(s) they have requested for. These differential services may include, specialised additional services not being rendered by competitors, fast and efficient services, around-the -clock availability to provide answers to clients consulting needs etc. whichever pricing strategy is adopted, industry (pricing) practice and client price adjustments are two key areas to consider before a choice is made.

4.   Industry practices

Depending on the practice in the industry, the fees or charges that are likely to be received in for instance by a recruitment or executive search agency who are paid based on whether or not their candidates are hired should be taken into consideration, in which case the practice is a payment to them of between 15 to 30 percent or more.

Adjusting Prices for Clients

When work is being done for certain clients, there may be a need for price adjustment to suit their budgets. These types of clients include Government, Large companies and small scale companies. It is quiet obvious that small companies cannot afford to pay the same price as large companies or government agencies. Consequently, billing may be based on the size of a company by having a low or a high price for them or a two price system. As a consultant, you may decide to adopt a two price system. However, you should remember that it is froth with problems but it also helps to eliminate a segment or range of clients that cannot afford to use your services.

Further, you should ensure that you conduct a market survey or investigation in order to have an idea of what others may be charging by asking other consultants to give you an idea about what they charge. What they say may

be the truth or partial truth; you should nevertheless conduct further investigations.

Other people to consult may include clients, editors
of relevant journals and trade or professional associations.
When all that has been said above are put together you
may well be on the way to determining what the professional fees should be.

How to Bill your client

A client may be billed in the following ways:

a.   Performance

This is a type of billing that is dependent on the ability
of the consultant to deliver expected or desired result. Consequently many consultants insist on

i.   Putting the agreement in writing
ii.   Not tying what they are to receive to profit.

An example of a performance contract includes agreeing to receive say, 15percent of every sale made or amount
saved as a result of a consultant's recommendations.

b.   Retainership

A retainership guarantees a consultant's place before
the client in that it is an agreement to give priority to a client for a certain number of hours during the month to help
tackle the problems that may emanate from the business
of the client from time to time within the month. It is a way
for to ensure a steady stream of income and the consultant
benefits in a month where there is less work or need for his
services.

Fixed Price

In a fixed price billing system the client is charged a fixed amount taking into consideration the amount of work to be done by the consultant. Whereas this type of billing may be beneficial to him, he will however, have to work hard to ensure that he covers or completes the work according to schedule to avoid using the time he would have spent rendering services to other clients on this project. A fixed price is charged having due regards to:

i.   The yearly overhead costs and direct expenses of business;
ii.   The labour cost of work undertaken.

Daily or Hourly

This involves billing clients the equivalent of a day's rate of work regardless of the number of hours or time taken up by the client in a particular day. In addition, the hourly rate is preferred by consultants who work part time as they seek flexible working hours to enable them attend to other clients or personal matters.

In summary whichever method of pricing or billing chosen, a consultant should be aware that it is advisable to be conversant with the different methods of calculating or billing as not all clients accept certain methods of billing. Consequently, what is acceptable to one client may not necessarily be applicable to another, which means that some clients such as Government agencies may even require a disclosure of the how the price was arrived at while others may just want a fixed price without bothering about how it was arrived at. The bottom line in all of these is to keep in mind that there are no static expectations from all clients. It is therefore your responsibility as a consultant to do what your clients seems to be comfortable with as long as it does not mean making you quote a lesser amount than you ordinarily would.

Promotion

Promotion includes all activities aimed at creating awareness for a product or service with the aim of convincing buyers to purchase. It involves the use of advertising, sales promotion, publicity, personal selling.

i.   Advertising

All company efforts aimed at bringing a product or service to the awareness of the general public or target market is referred to as advertising. Methods used in advertising include the print media such as newspapers and magazines, brochures, pamphlets etc. as well as the use of electronic media such as television, radio, internet and billboards to mention a few. Advertising when properly done has the advantage of keeping consumers constantly reminded of the existence and benefits derivable from the use of the products and services of a company.

For example adverts are now placed on buses, grocery carts, on walls of airport walkways, on train station walkways etc. In advertising there is a sponsor who is identified by the promotion of products and services. It needs to be mentioned that, it is usually a one-way medium of communication in that the sponsor tells the consuming public all it needs to know about its services. Advertising is also used for non-profit generating ventures such as creating awareness about the activities of political parties, religious activities among others.

ii.   Sales promotion

These are all non- personal promotional efforts geared towards deliberately increasing the quantity of a service by consumers. Media and other advertising methods are employed in order to increase and stimulate consumer demand for a specified period as well as address the problem of availability. The major targets for any sales promotion are usually the consumers and the distribution channels.

iii.   Consumer sales promotion

Consumer sales promotion is usually directed at consumers with the aim of increasing their consumption or the demand for a product or service. Companies employ various tactics like discounts, price slashes during festive seasons, prizes to be won by consumers who have shown loyalty by the quantity of a product or service purchased. Others include rebates and money back guarantees in the event the customer or client does not get value for money.

vi.   Trade sales promotion

Trade sales promotion is directed at wholesalers and retailers to encourage them to stock more of a producer's services. Some of these promotional packages include:

a.   Trade allowances-an incentive to encourage stocking of products.

b.   Dealer loader- these are incentives to encourage conspicuous display of a company's products and services.

c.   Training program- this involves training dealers' employees on how to get the best from a product or service.

Chapter 18
Creating Publicity for what you do

Publicity is a deliberate attempt by an organization or company to attract attention by creating awareness for its products and services through newspapers, magazines, television, billboards, radio talk shows internet websites etc. The benefit of a properly executed publicity is seen from its ability to capture the interest of the target audience in such a manner that an advert may not be able to because it tends to be regarded as more believable compared to other forms of advertisement.

The Remaining 3P's of Marketing

In the last chapter we discussed the 4 P's of marketing. Three other P's that were not mentioned directly are now expatiated upon:

a.   Process

Process refers to the steps or procedures required to get a product or service delivered on schedule. For instance when a customer orders snacks from a restaurant and it is delivered within say, 3 minutes, one could say that there is an efficient process in place as a result of the timely and efficient rendering of service by the restaurant.

Process is a fundamental ingredient in ensuring that consumers receive their orders within the agreed stipulated time or days. Any company that is able to factor in this important requirement for succeeding in the market place will have satisfied customers or clients who are likely to show loyalty and confidence in the company thereby leading to more patronage and spreading of the word to other potential clients who come in contact with them.

b.   People

People refer to the caliber of staff that is employed to do the work of the organization. Inappropriate and inadequate staffing is a minus which has therefore necessitated manpower training or capacity building is now an integral part of many business or organizational development processes. Clients and customers make judgments on the organizations based on the quality of staff they interact with as these leave lasting impressions on the clients who more or less make decisions based on their observations whether to continue doing business with the company or move somewhere else where their ego and feelings of importance will be better respected.

There is therefore a requirement that employees display appropriate interpersonal skills and aptitude and to also know how to provide what the client requires because consumers are very cardinal to any marketing effort. In the first place a company cannot have products without considering who is going to use them. Hence, any company that does not wish to see its investment come to nothing should understand the importance of the client in its agenda because it is the client that keeps it in business.

By the same token the needs and even wants of the client must be considered by talking to him to get to understand what he wants before making or producing the product or service. Anything short of this could spell disaster for the company as is often the case before now when companies thought that they were the one's better placed to determine what the consumer or client desires. On the contrary, research has shown that these actually know what they want and are ready to give up their loyalty to any company if other companies can provide what they want.

c.   Physical evidence

Physical evidence is used in relation to the kind of environment that the client meets in the process of transacting business with an organization. The client has expectations in the sense that he wants to see a well catered environment that is clean and inviting that will make him feel at home. Thus, consumers also make decisions based on what they can physically see and this goes a long way to determine whether they will keep on patronizing a company or not.

Distribution-Getting Service to Clients

Distribution is the process of getting products and services to client's through channels that are feasible and appropriate to a business. More often than not there is usually a middleman between the producer and the retailer. Consequently, a channel is required to get the service to the point where the consumer can easily access them with minimal efforts.

Products are shipped to a distributor who must have the confidence of the manufacturer having met the stipulated requirements for becoming a distributor who in-turn delivers the products to the sellers who again use their own channels to get to the consumers. For distribution to be effective there must be appropriate channels to use in order to get them to the consumers or clients on time. Below are some of the channels for getting products to the consumers.

i)   Advertisement—often used for consumable products and services.

ii)   Direct sales- through the use of the internet, via mail orders, telephone etc.

iii)   Wholesaler or distributor-this sells to the retailers.

iv)   Retailer—This sells to the consumers.

v.   Movement of companies in the value chain

When goods or services are produced and delivered to the distributor, along the line until the products or services get to the consumers, there is usually an added value by the handlers of the products or services at each point in the value chain. When the products get to the distributor and to the retailer, each of these add their own percentage, mark-up or margin on the products or services which is actually a reflection of the value- added in respect of expenditures on marketing, warehousing, transportation etc. In order to reduce the amount that the end consumer will be required to pay, some companies like Dell and Hewlett Packard have developed avenues for getting products direct to consumers thereby reducing the price that will be paid eventually by the end users.

vi.   Provision of bundled solution

Rather than expend money on individual products or services; producers are now grouping products and services in such a way that there can be shared costs in terms of distribution, support, and information for a package price.

Thus, producers are themselves involved in providing services to consumers of their products.

vii.   Emergence of new classes of clients

Some products or services are meant for a certain class of people. For instance when computers were first produced, they were meant for business use but along the line, Apple computers opened up the spread of usage to include home and individuals through the introduction of a graphical and user-friendly interface.

viii.   Re-packaging and re-introduction of old services

Some products or services never die as the producer's seek out new ways of making them appear like new. This may involve re-designing, re-packaging and changing channels of distribution. This new value added allows the owner not only to increase the prices, but to also seek out new customers or clients and consequently charge higher than normal prices for their products and services.

Marketing Plan and Why it is Important

A marketing plan is a conscious and deliberate effort by a company at identifying and stating clearly what it intends to do, where it intends to be at a certain stage of its existence and also what it intends to produce. As a consultant, your marketing plan can be as elaborate as a 75 page document or as small as a one page document that briefly encapsulates all your company wants to do and achieve. The following are the essential elements of a good one- page -marketing or business plan for your consulting business.

i)   Purpose- Deals with the reason for being in existence. That is, your objective for being in business. Without purpose there can be no direction, hence your company must define why it is in business and what it seeks to achieve.

ii)   Benefits- Your company should be able to state in succinct terms how its products or services will benefit the users or consumers in terms of the satisfaction derivable from such usage.

iii) Clients- The kind of clients likely to purchase your products and services needs to be defined to help engender focus and proper utilization of your company's resources. In this regard, your company needs to answer the questions; who is our client and what strategies are to be put in place for building a long-term relationship with him?

iv)   Niche- A niche market as stated in the previous chapter, is what your business has being able to carve out for itself. It is created where your company is able to identify a market it can excel in as well as have the advantage of the 'first mover' where it is able to determine and control the market by virtue of the 'niche' market it has been able to create for itself.

v)   Tactics- Tactics refers to the specific marketing tools to be used in reaching the client. These tools will form the basis on which your company navigates the murky waters of surviving and penetrating the market place.

vi)   Budget- It is your company's responsibility to determine the amount of resources in money, materials, human resource terms etc. that will be required to propagate its plans. The company needs to be explicit on how much it is willing to allocate to this effort.

Branding Products and Services

The word 'brand' has been defined by the American Marketing Association (AMA) as, a name, sign, symbol or design or a combination of them intended to identify the products and services of one seller or group of sellers from the others. Branding is important in that it keeps a company's product or service in the hearts and minds of the consumer which therefore requires research and development to ensure that the consumer continues to see the values he has hitherto enjoyed not decreasing, but rather increasing in value in their opinion. Thus, any company intending to win in the brand war needs to ensure that it builds on its promises to clients to provide unrivalled products and services that are unbeatable by any other and that have value for money.

Thus, a company needs to promote and protect its brand image jealously to be able to retain its clients. A good product or service will seek to achieve a clear delivery of its message; motivation of the buyer to purchase, ensuring client satisfaction and loyalty, getting the consumer or client's to be emotional about the product or service, thereby confirming its credibility etc. In addition, to win the brand war a company has to ensure that it 's meeting the needs and wants of the consumer or client and that it communicates this at every given opportunity that comes its way as part of it brand strategy for ensuring its pride of place in the market.

Direct and Indirect Marketing

Direct marketing is a form of product awareness or technique whereby companies and organizations advertise their products and services via ads in papers, magazines, online and on radio. It also takes advantage of direct mail operations and the cold calling method. Direct marketing is aimed at getting the owners of a product or service involved in the whole process of creating public awareness for them.

Personal Selling

Personal selling involves the delivery of a specially designed message to a prospect by a seller usually in the form of:

i)   Face to face selling;
ii)   Telephone and conferencing interface sales.

It also involves attempting to sell a product of high value where the usefulness of the product or service is explained in depth to the client to enable him or her make the decision to purchase. Making the sales may not be the only objective of the salesperson but rather bringing the product/service of the company to the awareness of the prospective client. Though it will be in the interest of the salesman to make the sales, and also in the interest of the buyer to seek enjoyment of the product or service at a reasonable price, it is not always the objective to achieve a sale as it were, by all means.

Further, because personal selling involves face-to-face contact with the prospective client, it is often considered to be more effective than other forms of sales promotion because the salesperson gets an immediate feedback from the client and is able to respond to the needs and wants of the client with suggestions for the appropriate product or service that will meet those needs.

One disadvantage of personal selling is the accusation by companies seeking to promote their brand that some salesmen undercut them by selling their products and services for higher prices than stipulated and then short-changing the company thereby making the brand look very expensive before the consumer who may eventually switch to complementary products and services in the event they perceive the company's products and services as being way out of their league. Salesmen who succeed in this endeavour are those that concentrate on meeting the needs and wants of the client, although salespeople have also been accused of improper behaviours that are to say the least annoying.

Indirect Marketing

Indirect marketing involves the use of third parties to market or sell a product or service. It is a more passive strategy compared to direct marketing strategy and often occurs through a not so aggressive means like the direct form of marketing. More often than not, it does not involve a specific product or even a goal. The objective is not to work at pushing a product intentionally on a prospective client but seeking out ways to perform a number of related activities, such as participating in community events, writing articles for publication, engaging in public speaking events and posting blogs on the internet. By this token those who have had the most benefits from a company's services help to disseminate information about their experiences with the company's products and services. Other ways an organization or company (including your consulting company) can indirectly market its products or services include participation in activities such as:

i)   Teaching in community or national workshop;
ii)   Holding city offices or serving on boards or committees;
iii)   Volunteering;
iv)   Speaking to other businesses at local events;
iv)   Demonstrations;
v)   Trade shows;
vi)   Sponsorships.

Premiums

Premiums are another way of reaching target clients and are inscriptions of a company's logo or promotional messages on items that are likely to be needed by clients, such as: calendar, baseball caps, calculators, mouse pads, t-shirts, pens and pencils, balloons etc. Proper planning in advance is required in order to ensure that the benefits derived by a company are worth the investment in this type of promotion.

Guerrilla Marketing

The use of unconventional tactics in order to achieve a conventional goal is what is referred to as guerrilla marketing. Profit or joy is the primary goal of the organization or business and as such will use every legal means such as investing energy instead of finance to achieve it. In order to achieve success in this endeavour, the marketer makes use of:

1.   The rule of thirds—this means that one third of a company's online marketing budget should be employed in the design and posting of its website, another one third should be used for promoting the web-site offline

and yet another one third should be set aside for improvement of the website by ensuring it is up-to-date, and entertaining for its readers and clients.

2. The rule of the ruler—the ruler is the owner or manager of a company and he is required to be actively involved and to take responsibility for the overall marketing effort instead of sitting on the sidelines.

3. The rule of twice—this rule is an admonition to be conservative in one's expectations of reward by remaining competitive all the way and realizing early that it may probably cost much more than initially envisaged to carry out marketing efforts online.

4. The 1/10/100—this rule advocctes that a company should invest more in its employees who are the primary points of contacts for clients, in this way a dollar spent on training and preparing them for the market place is likely to be the equivalent of $10 expended on communicating about the trade, which is also equivalent to $100 spent communicating with its clients.

5. The 10/30/60 rule- this requires a company to set aside 10 percent of its time and budget to talking to all in its marketing environment or universe. 30 percent of the budget should be dedicated to convincing and scouting for new clients who fall within its target market. Lastly 60 percent of the marketing budget should go to efforts geared towards retaining the loyalty of present clients. This means that the company will be able to make more profit at a lower cost as a result of concentrating its resources on its present client base.

Chapter 19
Use of IT, computers & the Internet

A Computer is a high-speed device used for facilitating productivity in the office. It is a machine that is used in manipulating data to produce information. It is also used for storage of information and data and is generally composed of a hardware and software element.

Information is the end result of manipulated data which gives the result of a research or finding. Information is required to be able to do any meaningful activity or achieve desired results. For instance, the reason you are reading this book is to seek information or find out certain things you wish to know about computers and the business of consulting. The word information has been employed in different ways without proper consideration to the meaning it may generate as it is often used synonymously with information technology. Other words that have been generated as a result are:

a. Informatics
b. Information age
c. Information societies
d. Information Science
e. Computer Science

Data on the other hand is the raw material required to produce information. It is the data which when properly manipulated within certain parameters of instructions that produces the desired result, referred to as information. It is usually the result of experience, observation or experiment or a set of premises such as numbers, words, or images with particular emphasis on measurement or observations of a set of variables.

Information age and Information Technology

In today's business environment a measure of technology is required for the survival of any business or organization that desires growth to the full potentials of its industry. Information depicts availability of knowledge as the ability to process data with ease leads to the generation of information that in turn provides knowledge for unraveling and solving all kinds of complex problems faced by individuals and organizations. Consequently, computers have found a wide usage among businessmen, accountants, lawyers, consultants, distributors, and producer's to mention a few.

What would it cost to acquire a standard technology for personal or business use?

It is possible to incur large expenditures in order to put the most up-to date technology in place, especially by companies with large budgets and the wherewithal to undertake these expenditures. However it may not be necessary to spend more than is necessary on obtaining the relevant technology that will suit the business. For one, what is relevant and up to date is what works well for a person or an organization. What is really required for the business is some basic application software to run the business.

In doing this however care must be taken to ensure that what is acquired is in consonance with what is acceptable and compatible with most of the other technologies in the industry one operates in.

Hardware

1.   Desktop computers

There are various makes of computers out there. Some of the most popular personal computers are the IBM's and IBM compatibles, and Apple's Macintosh. These have undergone more improvements so much so that program developers for IBM based applications have now brought it to a position of comparable advantage with that of Apple through the ingenuity of Microsoft's Windows applications.

When people purchase a computer they are looking to be able to navigate and discover how to use its many features. Apple computers are regarded as offering its buyer's standard desktop features and applications. However, it will appear that more and more people employ the use of personal computers in several countries than they use Apple computers and applications. Perhaps a basic reason for this could be as a result of the inexpensive and easy to find, understand and use nature of the PC's.

It needs to be mentioned that the type of computer purchased is irrelevant if it is cost effective. They all are basically configured through the same methodology or technology to manufacture each of the brands in the market place.

The following features are advisable for any one interested in owning a PC or Apple Computer: DVD writer, CD, Disk capacity, Memory.

LAPTOP (Note-books)

A laptop is so called because of the ease of movement and the ability to use and carry cbout. A laptop is really a desktop computer, which can be carried around but is smaller and likely to be more expensive. In other words, a laptop can conveniently perform the entire task a desktop can and comes with the convenience. There are different makes of laptops or notebooks as they are often called and the one chosen will be based on the features and design being sought for as well as the budget for it.

Printer

A printer is a device, which is used to produce a hard copy of documents. There are many types of printers but they can be basically categorized into LaserJet's and Inkjet printers. Depending on the size of a company whether already in business and doing well or just starting, whichever is chosen to be employed or purchased will produce an output that will meet set goals and expectations as they are sometimes difficult to differentiate between the two.

Fax

A fax unlike a printer is useful for sending documents at short notice to clients or for sending documents that can with the aid of a printer be produced as a hard copy to enable the receiver obtain an exact replica of the document sent. These days, there are internet fax services that allow users to transact their business. Users are given fax numbers that are tied to an e-mail account, which enables the receiver enjoy the benefit of receiving fax messages through a fax machine as well as through the e-mail box.

Scanners

Scanners enable reproduction, saving or copying to the computer system any document to be sent to clients or business partners. Printers have now been standardized to incorporate multi-features of printing as well as fax and scanning devices. However, scanners can be purchased as a sole item for the sole function of scanning alone.

CD, DVD's or external hard drives can be used to back up the documents or pictures from the camera or even copies of pictures that have already taken among the collections once scanned.

Softwares

Software's are application packages that aid the use of computers in communication. In today's high tech world of fast processing, retrieval and storing of information, the following applications packages among others are useful.

i.   Word processors

These are used for processing documents and they come in different forms. E.g. Word perfect, Linux packages & MS word which seems to be the standard.

ii.   Spreadsheets

Spreadsheets enable the user to manipulate tabulations in such a way that large documents which require extensive fields can be captured on a page at once. Hence, spreadsheets are used for calculations as they help to facilitate and simplify the processes invo ved because of the availability of formulae for easy manipulations. Some examples of spreadsheets include lotus 1-2-3 and MS Excel, which is the standard for spreadsheets today.

iii.   E-mails

E-mails can be used for several functions such as communication with friends, clients, business partners etc. E-mails are widely used and popular today and individuals and organizations employ the use of e-mails because of its ease and fast delivery of letters and business communications.

Examples of e-mails include:

a.   Free emails- which are freely available to everyone that seeks them.

b.   Quasi free e-mail- usually offered by web hosting companies on purchase of a web- hosting plan. This plan comes with the ability to host a website.

c.   Client based e-mails-this type is mainly used by companies who seek to have security of document and communications within and outside their own organizations. They do this by having their own server, which ensures that all emails leaving the corporation are stored on the corporate e-mail server. This also ensures that all e-mails received from other individuals and companies undergo thorough scanning for viruses and also enable them store the e-mails for legal reasons.

d.   Wireless e-mails- is usually done through the cell phone or PDA. At the moment corporations are the main beneficiaries of this technology but with time it is expected to spread to other users as it is still in the developmental stages.

e.   Back up and recovery

This goes hand-in- hand with anti-virus software's and is used to automate or store important data files at least forthnightly or weekly.

Data can be lost:

i.   When anti-virus software's fail to cetect or stop viruses from infecting files.

ii.   When an intruder gains access into a computer.
iii.   When installed software is incompatible with the operating system it could corrupt and crash the system.

iv.   When the installed hardware is such that it can corrupt the system.

v.   When the computer develops problems and thereafter crashes.

Data can be stored on CD or DVD as back-up to forestall loss.
Closely related to anti-virus software's are pop-up blockers that help to prevent unwanted materials and viruses from affecting the computer. In getting the pop-up and anti-virus blocker, it is wise to ensure that:

i.   It is able to auto scan the virus before it affects the computer;

ii.   It can automatically up-date itself to tackle new virus threats.

iii.   It has ability to scan e-mails for new virus threats;

iv.   It has ability to stop pop-ups, spywares, and adware types of virus threats.

v.   It should be able to stop all kinds of viruses as well scan instant messages downloads for viruses.

vi.   The company producing this software package should be able to provide online information to assist clients to learn more about current virus threats.

Why having a website helps

Having a website enables services to be rendered to clients quickly and cost effectively. As a consultant, you do not need to spend a lot of money as the case was some years ago as there are authoring software's that can enable you to easily build your own website. There are also web-designing templates to help you achieve this at reasonable cost.

Researching the internet

Like the catalog index card in a conventional library which aids in locating books, magazines, articles etc. to do this on the Internet the use of the search engines are indispensable.

The search engines have capacity for searching and producing far more results than can be found in a conventional library. For instance, where about 80,000 results are found in a conventional library, about 120,000,000 can be found for the same topic using the internet search engines.

Below are some useful search engines
Yahoo!:http://www.yahoo.com
Lycos: http://www.lycos.com
Google:http://www.google.com
Msn: http://search.msn.com

Altavista:http://www.altavista.ccm

Search Engines Watch:http://www.searchenginewatch.com

Bibliography

Although some of the underlisted references are out of print, they are nevertheless still useful and may be found in a library or store near you.

1. Amar Bhide et al; Harvard Business Review on Entrepreneurship, by Harvard Business School, Press.

2. Andersen TR, Zeltich .Jr; A Basic Course in Statistics,

3. Published by Holt Rhinehart and Winston Ruc.

4. Andy Bruce et al; Strategic Thinking, Published by Dorling Kinderly Limited.

5. Black, EP; Statistics, New York: Wesley publishing company

6. Clelland, R; Statistics for Business, London: Macdonald and Evans Ltd Page 53

7. Deborah J. Lucas et al; Inside the Mind—Textbook Finance, Published by Aspatore, www.Aspatore.com

8. Donald J. Trump; How to Get Rich, Ballantine Books Published by the Random House Publishing Company.

9. Goope H. et al (1952), A Guide to Business Statistics, New York, Cassell ltd page, 57.

10. Harper, U.G; Research   Methodology, carlifornia, and Dickson publishing company incorporated, page 53.

11. Kathleen Allen et al; The Complete MBA for Dummies, Published by Wiley Publishing Inc. 111 River Street Hoboken, NJ 07030. www.wiley.com

12. Ndagi J.T; Business Statistics and Statistical Methods, Cassell ltd, page 54.

13. Timothy R V Foster; How to Succeed as an Independent Consultant, Published by Kogan Page 120 Pentonville Road, London N1 9JN www.Kogan-Page.co.uk www.harpercollins.com

14. Jack Welch; Winning, Published Harper Collins, www.JackWelchwinning.com

15. Jeffery E. Garten; The Mind of the CEO, Published by Persus Publishing, East

16. Herb Cohen; You Can Negotiate Anything, Published by Bantam books, 1540 Broadway, New York, New York, 10036.

17. Peter F. Drucker et al; The Daily Drucker, Published by HarperCollins, Inc, 10 East 53rd Street, New York, NY 10022.

18. Rohan Hall; Stop Working! Published by Eye Contact Media Inc. Printed in the United States of America.

19. Randy Charles Epping; A Beginners Guide to the World Economy, Published by Vintage Books, New York www.vintage books.com.

20. Stephen Sharang; Administration of a Business: Growth Strategies for the Development and Survival of Today's

Corporate Organizations, Printed in USA by BookSurge Publishing, an Amazon Company.

21. Stephen Sharang; Managing Public Organisations: Understanding Financial Reporting and Policy Making in Government, Printed in Great Britain, by LuLu Publishing Company.

22. Steven Silbiger; The Ten Day MBA, Harper Collins Publishers

23. William A.Cohen; How to make it Big as a Consultant, by AMACOM Books, NY 10019. www.amacom.com

Some Useful Websites

1. http://www.isixsigma.com/dict onary/Customer_Focus-8.htm
2. http://www.scu.edu/ethics/practising/decision/whatisethics.html
3. http://slu.edu/depts/International_Business/conc.html
4. http://www.sba.gov/smallbusinessplanner/index.html
5. http://www.entrepreneur.com/articles
6. http://goinglobal.com/hot_topics/Sweden_hanson_global.asp
7. http://www.time-management-guide.com/planning.html
8. http://www.sptimes.com/News/032901/NIE/who_is_an_entrepreneur.shtml
9. http://www.wisegeek.com/what -is -a-contract.htm
10. http://www.quickmba.com/law/org/
11. http://en.wikipedia.org/wiki/negotiation
12. http://www.imanet.org/about_ mcnagement.asp
13. http://www.ca.courses-careers.com/management.htm
14. http://www.netmba.com/marketing/mix/
15. http://education.yahoo.com/reference/dictionary/entry/enthusiasm
16. http://www.tsl.state.tx.us/ld/tutorials/professionalism/IA.html
17. http://dictionary.reference.com/browse/objective
18. http://en.wikipedia.org/wiki/Research_and_development
19. http://education.yahoo.com/reference/dictionary/entry/packaging

20. http://education.yahoo.com/reference/dictionary/entry/administration
21. http://dictionary.reference.com/browse/skill
22. http://dictionary.reference.com/browse/competence
23. http://www.koganpage.com/products/the-top-
24. consultant/BusinessandManagement/B/Management_Consulting/

INDEX

Access to additional capital 24
Accessibility 42
Accountants 146
Accountability 91
Active partner 22
Additional paperwork and government regulations 26
Administration 35
Advertising 32, 179, 185,
Analyzers 139
Anger 67, 73,75
Alternate contact person 62
Areas where Benchmarking should focus on 116
Assistance in decision making 23
Attorney 146-147

Back up and recovery 204-206
Bank Account 6
Banks and financial institutions 6
Benefits 7, 10, 34
Benefits of Six-Sigma to a Business 125-128
Benefits of TQM 120
Black or white boards 167
Blueprint 2, 94
Body language 57, 59, 71
Boss 4, 20, 44
Board of directors 26
Bondholders 85
Brainstorming 39
Budget 93, 111, 117, 123

Business Angels 46-47
Business sense 3

Candor 11
Capital 14, 17, 19
Characteristics of the Control Process 112
Choice of name of a business 15
 Clear cut goals and objectives 12
Clients 120, 121, 127
Client based e-mails 204
 Client satisfaction 13, 121, 127, 160
Common Thread 66
Companies and Allied Matters Act 3
Competitors 10, 67, 78
Computer 160, 167, 168
Computer Presentations 167-168
Computer Science 199
Consistent deficiency in supply 10
Consultant 10, 17, 18, 29
Consumer sales promotion 186
Co-ordination of all parts of a business 13
Corporate Affairs Commission 4
Corporate Scandals 87, 92
Cost 38, 41, 56
Cost contracts 154
Contract risks 150
Creativity 3, 123
Credibility to clients in industry 25
Creditors 20, 85
Cultural Relativism 82, 83
Customize Service 176

Daily or Hourly 184
Debt (Preference Shares) 46
Deliver a service 5
Delegation of duties 106

Departmentation 105-106
Desktop computers 201
Design 202, 206
Disposal of Assets 43
Divide and conquer 68
Division of labour 105
Doppel-Ganger 66
Dormant partner 21
Drive or interest 12
Duration 16, 23, 41, 142, 151

Economy Criteria 111
Effectiveness Criteria 111
Efficiency Criteria 110
Ego trip 5
Elements required in any contract 156-157
E-mails 204, 205
Employees 11, 14, 16
Entrepreneur 1, 3, 138
Enthusiasm 162
Environmentalists 86
Executive board of directors 86
Expectancy 99
Expertise 2, 20, 31, 30, 44
External Sources of Data 55-56
Equipment 122, 124, 135
Equity 7, 42, 45
Ethics 77, 79

Face to face selling 194-195
Fairness 77, 91
Feelings 73, 80
Fax 202, 203
Finance and Accounting firms 32
Finding the right caliber of staff 107
Fixed Price 153, 155, 184

Fixed price contracts 153
Flip charts 168
Formal contract 152, 153
Formation and incorporation of companies 3
Free emails 204
Fresh ideas 16
Functionally specialized firms 32

Gearing 42
General 42, 45
General management 17, 33
Government 33, 35, 56
Gross profit 146
Guilt or regret 75

Handouts 166-167
High Overhead 15
High price 180, 181, 182
Hygiene Theory 99
Hobby, Interest, Talent 44

Ideal proposal 142-143
Immediate community 86, 91
Importance of benchmarking 116
Implied contracts 150
Incentive contract 155
Income taxes 26
Inadequate accounting records 13
Industry practices 182
Industry specific firms & the so called think tank 33
Inefficiency in inventory management 14
Information 65
Informatics 200
Information age 200
Information societies 200
Information Science 200

Insight 3, 10, 23
Instrumentality 98
Integrity 107
Intelligence 108
International operations 35
Interview 50-51
Internal Secondary Data Sources 55
Investment on fixed assets 14

Key steps to successful benchmarking 115

Letter contract 152
Lack of properly written or documented business plan 9
Lack of information about competitors 10
LAPTOP (Note-books) 201-202
Loans from Bank 47
Leadership 95
Legal requirements 3, 20, 41
Labour 3, 63, 105
Land 1, 43, 44, 77
Level of influence of participants 62
Limited 22
Limited liability partner 22
Law 79
Low Hanging Fruit 66
Lose-lose 64
Lose-win 64
Low morale and overworking of staff 9
Low price 180-181
Low Revenue 15

Machinery 3, 124, 126
Make money 4, 5, 173
Management firms 32
Management skills 32
Manufacturing 34

Maturity 108
Meet-the -competition strategy 181-182
Mental rehearsal or creative visualization 169
Mission statement133-134
Mis-management 10, 11
Money 167, 172, 173, 181, 186
Motivation 193

Natural laws 84
Naïve Relativism 82-83
Negative Emotions 74
Need to find new sources of Capital 17
Need to keep abreast of government regulations as they affect a business 17
Need for computers and IT 18
Need to improve efficiency 17
Need to restore a system 18
Need for training & capacity building 18
New classes of clients 191
Niche market 175, 192

Observation 188-200
Offer and acceptance 150
Online statement 6
Order agreement 152
Ordering 114
Organization 164-165
Origin of TQM 120
Overdrawing capital for personal use 14
Overflowing Cup 67
Overhead transparencies 167

Packaging 34
Patience 68
People 188
Performance 183

Performance contracts 154-155
Personnel 16
Personal Savings 42
Physical evidence 189
Place or (Placement) 179-180
Planning 94
Practice 165
Price 180
Printer 202
Professionalism 163
Purpose 114
Purchase order 152-153

Poor Business Skills 16
Potential organizational disputes 24
Power 64
Pride 75
Principle on Which TQM is Based 121-124
Problem of company politics 18
Process 187-188
Procurement and purchasing 34
Production 1, 3, 10
Products 10, 15, 17
Products and Services 171, 177, 179
Prospectors 138
Provision of bundled solution 190
Psychologist 66
Public sector firms 33

Qualities of a Prospective Employee 107
Quasi free e-mail 202
Questionnaires 52-53

Rationale 114
Reason for writing a proposal 141
Re-packaging and re-introduction of old services 191

Retailer 190
Retainership 183
Regional and local firms 33
Rehearsals 169
Religion 78
Research and development 34
Responsibility 91
Retained Earnings 43
Revenue and Customs Authorities 19
Right perception 176
Risk 2, 9, 181
Rising increases in service cost 9
Reward 73, 84, 99
Robot 67
Roles 114
Role Relativism 82
Rule of thirds 196
Rule of the ruler 197
Rule of twice 197

Sales promotion 186
Scanners 202-203
Shareholder activism 92
Shop 2, 113, 193,
Skill 2, 16, 17, 18
Shareholders 85
Societal expectations 79-80
Sole practitioners 33
Span of control 106
Specialist 1
Specialty firms outside of business 33
Specialized services 35
Spreadsheets 203
Strategy 32, 33, 63
Strong contracts 149
Structure 115

Sufficient capital 12

Tactics 192
Target market 13, 15, 33, 197
Tax liabilities 19, 22
Telephone book 3
Terms of Employment in Bureaucratic Organizations 108-109
Terms of agreement 141
Term structure of interest rates 42
Time 42, 43, 50, 52
Trial Balloon 68
Trade sales promotion 186
Training and Apprenticeship 44
Transparency 91

US Bureau of labour and statistics 3
US Bureau of Census's Basic Monthly Survey 3
Universalism 84
Utilitarianism 84

Vacation and sickness stability 24
Valence 98
Value statements 133
Venturing 1, 5
Verbal Contracts 153
Vision statement 132
Visual aid 166

Weak contracts 149
Win-lose 64
Wireless e-mails 204
Whipsaw Auction 67
Wholesaler or distributor 190
Word processors 203
Worry and disappointments 44
Working capital 43

Appendix

Please send me your success stories. I would like to know how the information in this book has helped you as I look forward to hearing from you. Kindly, mail your stories to: stephensharang@yahoo.com

About the Author

Dr. Sharang's experience comes from years of research and work in the private and public sectors in the fields of Management, Finance and Accounting and their application to a real world scenario as to be helpful to all who manage public or corporate organizations.

He is a member of the following professional bodies among others:

• Nigerian Institute of Management• Association of National Accountants of Nigeria• International Academy of Business, Michigan State University, USA • International Academy of Management, London UK; where he is a Fellow•

Dr. Stephen Sharang, CPA, is the Finance Attaché/ Financial Consultant of the Embassy of Nigeria, Brussels, Belgium, where he currently, lives.

www.ingramcontent.com/pod-product-compliance
Lightning Source LLC
Chambersburg PA
CBHW071410170526
45165CB00001B/231